I CAN PRAY,
YOU CAN PRAY

I CAN PRAY, YOU CAN PRAY

A Worldly Approach to Spirituality

RICHARD W. CHILSON

David McKay Company, Inc.
New York

To Matthew
        May he live forever.

Copyright © 1978 by Richard W. Chilson

Library of Congress Cataloging in Publication Data
Chilson, Richard.
    I can pray, you can pray.
    Bibliography: p.
    Includes index.
    1. Prayer. I. Title.
BV210.2.C5   248'.3   78-6553
ISBN 0-679-50860-0

1 2 3 4 5 6 7 8 9 10

Manufactured in the United States of America

Contents

PART ONE: *The Principles of Prayer*

Chapter One: *Making A Start* _____ 1
The Spiritual Marketplace 1; An Examination of Motives 4;
What Do I Want From This Book? 4; Is This the Time? 5; For
and Against Praying Now 6; Taking Stock 8; How to Use This
Book 12

Chapter Two: *The Pleasure Principle: Enjoy Your Prayer* _____ 14
The Experience of Saints 15; Inertia 16; Toward Self-Motivation 18; Distractions 18; Scheduling a Time to Pray 19

Chapter Three: *The Work Principle: Be Serious* _____ 20
A Fallen Life 20; Pleasure Needs Working On 21; Creating a
Schedule 22; The Prayer Contract 25

Chapter Four: *The Experimental Principle: Be Open* _____ 26
A Time to Decide 27; A Meditation On the Breath 28; Medita-
tion Posture and Meditation on the Breath 28; Meditation on the
Attention 30

Chapter Five: *The Imaginative Principle: Be Original* _____ 32
Poverty of Pornography 33; A Challenge to See 34; Meditation
of the Thousand-Petaled Lotus 34

Chapter Six: *The Journal Principle: Keep a Record* _____ 36
A Yardstick to Measure By 36; On Using the Journal 37; Life
Diary 37; Dream Diary 38; Prayer Diary 38; Prayer Experi-
ence 39; Prayer Gifts 39

PART TWO: *Prayer Exercises*

Chapter Seven: *Cultivating Silence* _____ 41
Too Much Noise 42; The Noise Goes Inside 44; Silencing the
Noise 45; Meditation on Noise 46; The Porous Body 46;
Meditation to Music 47; Mantra Meditation 47; Being Silent
48

Chapter Eight: *Cultivating Concentration* _____ 49
Gentle but Firm 49; Temptations to Give Up 50; Avoid Judgments and Criticism 51; No Expectations 52; Concentration
Defined 53; Expanding Versus Narrowing 54; Meditation
with a Candle 55

Chapter Nine: *Cultivating Physical Peace* _____ 56

Why the Body? 56; Reclaiming the Body 58; Are We Ready
for Body Prayer? 58; The Journey as Guide 59; Centering 61;
Finding the Three Centers 62; The Body Never Lies 62; Centering Exercise 63; May the Force Be with You 64; The Energy Body 65; A Matter of Fine Tuning 66; Fasting and
Almsgiving 69; Developing Body Awareness 70

Chapter Ten: *Cultivating Spiritual Peace* _____ 72
Relaxation 73; A Relaxation Technique 75; Working on Consciousness 76; Ego Training 78; Discerning the Spirit 80

PART THREE: *The Experience of Prayer*

Chapter Eleven: *Music and Art* _____ 87
The Visual Arts 89; The Powers of Imagination 90; Praying with
Art and Music 92

Chapter Twelve: *The Prayer of Sports* _____ 95
Obstacles to Sports Prayer 95; Sports as Prayer 97; Walking
with Awareness 98; Tennis and Golf 98; Tai Chi and Mountain Climbing 98; Dance 100; Guidelines for Praying in
Sports 102

Chapter Thirteen: *Prayer as a Nature Walk* _____ 104
Walking Meditation 104; Be Attentive to the Walk 106; Open-
ing the Senses 107; Energy Fields 108; Work with a Camera 109;
Review of Experience 110; Creation of the Haiku 111

Chapter Fourteen: *Prayer as Story* _____ 112
Story and Religion 113; Stories That Teach 113; Initiation
Stories 114; Entering into the Story 116; Storytelling 117; Personal Parables 119; Remembering Dreams 120; Dream Interviews 121; Role Playing with Dreams 121; Expanding Dreams
122; Dream Collage 123; Life Stories 123; Autobiographical
Turning Points 125; Creating Stories 126; Poetry 127

Chapter Fifteen: *The Prayer of Persons* _____ 129
Mirror Meditation 129; Body and Sexuality 132; Massage 133;
Conversation and Listening 134; Dialogue 136

Chapter Sixteen:
  Epilogue _____ 138
  Bibliography _____ 144
  Index _____ 148

Acknowledgments

I would like to thank all the people who had a part in the creation and birth of this book: first of all, my teachers in worldly spirituality, especially Ken Ring, the most worldly of all; next, my friends and fellow travelers at Saint Thomas and Holy Spirit, especially Isabelle and Joan; and, finally, thanks to Mary Cross, who read it and encouraged me, to Nancy Midlin, who typed it, and to Walt Baxter, who proofread when I couldn't look anymore.

I

THE PRINCIPLES OF PRAYER

One

Making a Start

The Spiritual Marketplace

We live in a spiritual age. This is not a value judgment, simply an observation. Spirituality is in our culture today in ways we might have thought impossible just twenty years ago. We keep coming upon it in the most secular and unlikely circumstances.

Take airports for example: a few months ago, I had to fly to Los Angeles. As I entered the Oakland airport lobby, I was struck by a sign to the effect that some people were in the airport soliciting money for their religion. They felt they were allowed to engage in such activity under the First Amendment. But the airport, so the sign warned, did not support or endorse these groups.

I smiled, thinking of all the exotic followers of the Reverend Moon and Hare Krishna, and then forgot all about it as I continued my own business. But later, coming out of a magazine store, I was approached by a nice young woman who immediately pinned a flower on my shirt and asked where I was from. Pleasantly put off guard, I replied that I lived in Berkeley. "Oh," she said, "so do I. I teach school in Berkeley, and that's why I'm here. Our pupils desperately need textbooks, and so I'm out collecting money."

To myself, says I, that sounds like a worthy cause. She probably teaches at one of the poorer schools, and the cause sounds legitimate. So I handed her some money, and she, thanking me, in turn offered me a copy of her magazine. Only then did it dawn on me what had happened. I had just given money to Hare Krishna. In spite of the warning in the lobby, I'd been had, duped into giving money to a spiritual group that was masquerading as an ordinary secular cause sans sari, incense, or chanting.

The scent of spirituality has so invaded modern America that we often can't tell a spiritual discipline by its apparel. Transcendental Meditation is marketed like hamburgers rather than as a prayer; the Soko Gokai sect encourages its followers to pray for cars and wealth rather than for the will of God. Werner Erhard and his EST organization use tactics and language that would seem a crude, tasteless parody of the old-time revival until we realize with a shock that Werner is after the same goal as the August night revivalist: to get his audience to change their ways. We are in the midst of a spiritual renaissance in secular clothing.

All of a sudden, unfashionable words are in again—words such as *meditation, prayer,* and *spiritual work.* And of course books such as this one come along and capitalize on the new turn and claim to talk of prayer in worldly terms.

Just what is going on? Well, I can only speak for myself. But as a Roman Catholic priest, I have discovered much about the spiritual side of my being from the current revival. As in all mass culture, much of what is happening is superficial and, like too much else today, is merely another soon-to-be-obsolete product put onto the American market to make a buck. The packaging is slick and sometimes downright deceiving. But the reason for the package in the first place shouldn't be taken lightly: there is a genuine longing throughout our society today for the spiritual.

Our established churches have been found bankrupt, and many people assume that they are unable to fulfill this longing. So the entrepreneurs have moved in to market the East for American consumption. Much of what passes for spirituality today is really just a marketing device, and some people are being misled.

And our turn to the East, when it is not corrupted into some palatable Western mode, is often confusing. We don't possess these spiritu-

2

alities as a part of our upbringing. They're exotic and unusual; we're either enchanted or feel out of place. It's very hard, if not impossible, for a Westerner to understand in a full sense Tibetan Buddhism, Yoga, or even Zen.

As a Western priest, I have been greatly helped by these Eastern spiritualities. They have opened my eyes to another reality—another way of seeing. And coming back home, I have found a Western spirituality that is capable of the same developments as its Eastern counterparts, but which feels like home to me in a way that Buddhism never could.

I'm speaking of our need for roots. When we embark upon the spiritual path, we attempt—like plants—to grow toward the sky. But if our roots are not deep, they can't ground us securely and we'll only topple and die. Our American roots lie in the West. No matter how in love or fascinated with the East we may be, it will always remain exotic and extraordinary for us—something we ultimately do not know. There must be a way by which we in the West can make the spiritual journey along our own route.

In this book, we begin our journey from our own culture and history. Here is a way of learning to live as our ancestors have seen it and lived it. But this is not a book of Christian or Jewish spirituality. The spiritual insights from our religious traditions can be presented apart from their religious dress. So there is no need for you to affirm that there is a God or that Jesus is the Messiah in order to embark upon this experiment, just as you need not believe Gautama is the Buddha in order to begin Buddhist meditation.

I like to define prayer as the process that allows us to open up more and more fully to the whole of reality. This book is for those searching for a fuller life, for more reality. We sense that there is a richer dimension to living, and we would like to expand and cultivate this experience. The Western and Eastern spiritual traditions provide a way into that kind of living. We'll look at both of these great traditions to see how the East can complete and fulfill underdeveloped elements in our own tradition.

I invite you to enter into an experiment through this book. The numerous exercises provide a journey in discovery. Do the exercises and remain open to your experiences. Our experiences through such exercises gradually open us to and convince us of the reality of the spiritual dimension.

This book is for living, not for thinking. It is for those of us who yearn for something more. We're ready to set out in quest; we're not sure just what this something more is or looks like. But if we have the courage to begin, the journey itself will reveal to us the shape and dimensions of the spirit.

An Examination of Motives

Before we proceed any further, let's bring into the light the reasons for picking up such a book in the first place. Perhaps those reasons seem quite obvious and you believe you don't need to consider them.

Maybe you want to know about prayer from a worldly point of view. Perhaps you're intrigued that a book on prayer can call itself worldly. Or you want to learn how to pray. These may be the true reasons any of us have for picking up such a book. But let's look a little more closely anyway.

What Do I Want From This Book?

Right now take five or ten minutes to bring to mind your reasons for reading this book. Five minutes is not too long a time. True, during that time, you could finish reading this chapter and be that much more into your quest of gleaning from the book what you want. But if you take the time to bring into better focus your motives, the rest of your reading can be more economical. So after reading these directions, put the book down for a few moments of reflection before you continue.

Make yourself comfortable and relaxed. Close your eyes for a few minutes and turn your attention to your breathing. Observe the breath as it goes in and out of your body.

When you feel relaxed and recollected, ask yourself what you really seek from this book. Don't be too quick to answer. Allow the response to arise gradually out of your silence. Take some time to allow the response to explain itself in its fulless.

What does your response imply about the way you should read this book? Where do you want to be when you finish the book? What do you want to gain through the process of this experiment? Ask these questions of yourself now, and allow the answers to appear out of your silence.

Now that you have consulted yourself about your motives, let's expand upon them. First of all, there is obviously some need or lack we have felt in our life that prompts us to enter into the realm of prayer. Even if the reason for reading is mere curiosity, still it is significant that the curiosity is in the area of prayer rather than of music or philosophy, for example. Something is missing from our life, and we have an inkling that perhaps that missing dimension is related to prayer.

Perhaps our life is living us. We wonder where the time goes. It flies by so fast that we haven't had the chance to savor or enjoy the week before we're at the brink of another weekly round. On the other hand, we may be confronted by empty time—time that is hollow and cannot be filled with our usual preoccupations and distractions.

In one sense, the worst thing that can happen to us is the fulfillment of our dreams. As long as we're striving for something—be it a job, a degree, love, security, or leisure—we're motivated and our life has purpose. But when our dream becomes reality, our motivation and directive energy are fulfilled and satiated, and we are brought to a standstill. At this point, we might search for another dream to pursue, and if we're lucky, we'll never run out of dreams. But this constant living in the future doesn't seem to be the best way to spend a life. There must be a way of living that focuses upon the present, gaining motivation, satisfaction, and enjoyment from the here and now rather than upon the far-off dream of what could, should, or might be.

Living in the present is certainly not the way of routine and rat race. Routine prevents me from noticing the passing moment. Routine narcotizes me to what is really happening now. It is a lullaby crooned by a not-so-nice mother to keep her child somnolent and out of trouble. Rocked in loving arms with our eyes closed, we're yet aware deep down inside that we're entrapped and are missing all that is happening during our nap.

Is This the Time?

Granted your interest in prayer, is this the right time to embark upon a prayer experiment? It is guaranteed that simply reading another book on prayer will do nothing for anybody. The only way to deal with prayer is to pray. And to experiment with praying will take more time than reading this thin volume.

So let's again pause to examine the factors that are favorable or unfavorable to entering upon a prayer experience. This book has nothing to offer unless you're willing to put into practice the different exercises and experiments. If you have read this far without bothering to do the first exercise, then you should pause now to examine just why you didn't do it.

Perhaps it seemed too simple and obvious. After all don't we know why we read a book? Maybe you assure yourself that you'll stop and do the more difficult and exciting exercises. But will you? Who knows just what an experiment will produce before performing it? Do any of us really know ourselves that well? And if we do, then why waste time reading a book about something and someone we already know deeply?

Is time or laziness the reason? The experiments take time and will power. The time I suggest is about twenty minutes a day and one additional hour during the course of the week. In other words, your prayer work will demand three hours out of about 110 waking hours a week. Is that more than you can afford to give?

A more pointed question: Is that more time than you ordinarily waste in a week? One paradox we discover as we begin to pray is that prayer has some miraculous power to multiply time. When I take time to pray, I find that my day is much fuller and has more room for all my activities than when I skip prayer because I feel I have no time for it. It is on those days when I do not pray that I fail to accomplish what has to be done.

For and Against Praying Now

So let's examine the suitability of this present moment for prayer. For this exercise, you'll need a pencil and paper. Sit in a comfortable position and close your eyes. Observe your breath as it enters and leaves your body. Allow your breath to slow down your racing thoughts and bring a feeling of rest and peace.

After a few moments, when you feel recollected, begin the exercise. Ask yourself the reasons prompting you to begin a prayer experiment now. List these reasons on the lefthand side of your paper.

Then on the righthand side of the page, list the reasons against beginning a prayer experiment now. Take your time and let the reasons come to you out of your silence. Don't search or grasp after reasons; they will appear in due course. Take at least ten minutes for this exercise. Now!

If you can't bring yourself to do this exercise before continuing, then you know this time for you is not the right time to deal with prayer. There is nothing wrong with this situation—it is simply not your time. You can try again another day, and perhaps the time will be right for you.

If you have done the exercises, let's evaluate your time for prayer.

The exercise is very simple to evaluate. If you were able to take the time to do the exercise, you're ready now to embark upon the prayer experiment. In fact, you have already begun. The content of what you put on paper during the exercise is not important; what is important is that you have actually done the exercise.

But, you protest, what about all my reasons pro and con? Don't they have any significance? No, they do not. All of our reasons both pro and con are ultimately arbitrary and the work of some impish little monkey who lives within and tries to dominate our mind.

The truth is we need no more reasons for praying than for eating or sleeping. But with prayer our needs may not be as obvious to us as they are with eating and sleeping. Still we do have a need and drive for the self-transcendence and the expanded experience of consciousness that prayer provides. Once we recognize the need for prayer in our life—not because it will be good for us, or because someone says we should pray, or because we feel guilty about not praying, but because we realize we need to pray just as we need to sleep and eat—then we need reasons neither for nor against prayer.

But what about those reasons committed to paper? Are they truly reasons? Solid reasons? Or are they only rationalizations—arguments we construct to justify our behavior and ways of thinking? Reasons are not arguments; reasons are perceptions of reality that determine how we shall live.

Take the example of sleep. We sleep because our bodies need sleep. We don't sleep because it's a nice way to add variety to life's other activity of wakefulness. We don't sleep because we want to dream or because we think it's good to lie prone for several hours a day. We sleep because we need to sleep. It's the same with prayer. We pray because we need to pray.

What about those reasons against prayer right now? There is one valid reason for not praying. If it appears on your list, you should not embark upon the journey. The reason is "I do not want to pray now," and it usually appears as a failure to do the exercise itself. All other reasons against prayer are fabrications by that monkey within us that does not want us to pray. If you did the exercise or even if you are willing to do it now, that is sufficient reason to embark upon the journey.

Most other reasons are rationalizations. We don't have the time. But we'll never have more time than right now. Our days will never grow any longer. And if we worry that we're already overcommitted, we should examine how much time we waste. How much time do we wander about aimlessly? We think about what has to be done rather than simply doing it. We watch television programs we're not really interested in. Prayer might help us put the wasted time to good use, and chances are we'll gain time through prayer. For prayer will not occupy all the time we probably waste today.

Suppose I say I'm not ready or prepared for prayer? I could claim I must wait until my life is more stable and together. Or I have to wait until I know more about life or my religion before I can venture into prayer. Or I must wait until I can find a teacher or a guru who will help me personally. These are all rationalizations.

What would happen if we postponed sleep until our life was more stable and we could enjoy it more? Or if we had to know more about sleep and dreaming before we entered into it? And how many of us are really experts at falling asleep? It is actually something that we luckily fall into every night; we don't quite know how it happens. Very few of us must go to a sleep specialist in order to learn how to sleep.

The case is much the same with prayer, just a little more subtle. Indeed we will recognize, like the good person in Molière who discovers he has been speaking prose all his life, that we have been praying all our lives. We just haven't noticed it or taken advantage of it. We already pray, but now we want to use what we know more effectively. We wish to learn, not how to pray, but how to pray better, just as we might want to learn how to sleep better and take better advantage of our sleep. This is the journey we are really embarking upon.

And with our two exercises, we have already begun the journey. For they were not just exercises, they were prayer experiences. We have already prayed twice. What was it like? Was it enjoyable? The hardest task in beginning a journey is actually getting started. Where is the right place to start? What do I need in order to complete the journey successfully? And how do I start?

We can forget right now about all those questions and others like them. We're already on our way. We've started our journey from right here and now in our lives—the best and only place to begin from. We take with us only our own experiences and learning—the best and only equipment for the journey. And we commence our prayer experience by praying—the only way to begin. Bon voyage!

Taking Stock

At the start, we would all do well to examine just who we are and what we take with us on this journey. No one starts from a position of emptiness. We have all had experiences and practices in the life of

8

prayer, even if we never thought of them that way. Now we'll be building upon these life experiences and disciplines in a more conscious way, but we'll be building upon our own foundations nonetheless. So let's spend some time right now examining our baggage for the journey.

For this exercise you'll need a pen or pencil and three sheets of loose-leaf paper. As in the previous exercises, prepare yourself by getting comfortable and spending a few moments observing your breath.

The first page will concern our religious or spiritual experiences. What have been your spiritual peaks and valleys? If they are hard to recognize, perhaps you are looking at only the religious areas of your life. Or perhaps you don't think you've had spiritual experiences because you don't consider yourself religious. Such experiences are for the pious and the holy. But are you sure there have never been moments when you felt an overwhelming happiness—a happiness so great that it overflows the moment and allows your being to expand until you feel able to embrace and love everyone and everything?

Have there been times when you've been so involved in some work or action that you've completely lost the sense of yourself as doing the work. Instead there was simply the work doing itself, and you were a part of it. This has happened to me at times as I have been playing the piano. Suddenly during my playing, I become so involved in the music that I'm no longer conscious of playing. Rather I feel the music simply flowing, and I'm part of the music. I'm not making the music any longer; there is no longer any need on my part to try to hit the correct notes or to concentrate upon my playing; somehow I and the music have united, and the music flows from my being naturally. I and the notes have become one so that for the moment we no longer exist as separate entities, but rather there is a new creation—the music. This kind of experience happens as well in sports or even in work, and it is indeed a spiritual experience.

On the second sheet of paper, we want to catalogue our experiences of what religious language refers to as conversions. At this point in our exercises, we want to do no more than merely note these different experiences. Later as we work in our journal, we can flesh them out. Perhaps your conversion was a specifically religious one. You passed from one way and style of living to another.

But the experience of conversion is not limited to the obviously religious realm of being. A conversion as deep and powerful as the religious may occur in the secular sphere. Conversions occur often at crisis moments in our lives—times of trouble, turmoil, and confusion. Suddenly the way in which we have been living and thinking is no longer meaningful or satisfactory to us. We feel lost, bored, or aimless. Or worse: we feel as though we are dying, or at least that we cannot go on as we are. Then either suddenly or step by step, a new way of living presents itself to us, and we begin to see our life and our world through a different set of eyes. We have found a new vision, a new reason for living.

External periods in our life when we are ripe for conversion experiences include adolescence, when we must cope with the terrible task of growing from child into adult. Vocational decisions also trigger conversion experiences, particularly if the vocation will significantly affect our life style as, for example, the medical, ministerial, Peace Corps, or military vocations do. Similarly a person can usually find a conversion at the point of vocational change, particularly if the change is a major one—leaving teaching to enter the business world, leaving business to enter law. The fact that some professions such as medicine and teaching actually confer the title of doctor or professor shows the extent to which those professions believe they should affect people's lives. But in some way, every occupation affects us spiritually and determines how we perceive the world. Whenever there is a change in the way we perceive the world, we can say we have undergone a conversion. And no matter how small a change it is, it is a conversion. Take some time now to chronicle briefly the major conversion experiences in your own life.

Our experiences of healing also tend to be rich spiritual moments. The third sheet of paper is the place where we can briefly record these significant experiences. The time of sickness and recovery from illness is full of the possibility of a renewed vision and awareness of life. I become ill with irritating and annoying colds and flu at times when my body and spirit are overtaxed and overworked. The slogan "I am going to have a nervous breakdown. I have worked for it and I deserve it." is not far from right. Colds and minor sicknesses do not strike us by chance. Instead they often hit us when we need them—when it is time to take a few days off from the rat race, when we need to have impressed upon us once again that the world doesn't really need us for its successful functioning, when we need to be warned that our pace and style of life are not really healthy. At these times, along comes an involuntary vacation. And even if we refuse to give in and go to bed as our body is asking us to do, we nevertheless can't proceed as though everything were normal: the drippy nose, the stuffed-up head, the rasping throat see to that.

And consider the magic moment when the cold or fever breaks. It is glorious to be alive then; I feel a new lease on life. Health is the greatest gift in the world, and for a little while, I truly appreciate the gift. So in truth, this sickness has a positive side effect: it helps me to appreciate what I forget in the bustle of living. And this is exactly what any spiritual experience will do. It will help me become aware and appreciate the joy of simply being alive.

Serious illnesses and their cure are potentially even more open to this deeper insight and appreciation for life. Of course there is also the possibility that we may be blind to the opportunity implicit in illness. We may respond with only self-pity and depression. On the other hand, some people stricken with the most painful and horrible illnesses are among the most spiritual and even happiest people in the world. They truly appreciate life and are fully alive to the moments of life left to them. Can we call these people more unfortunate than others who will live many years longer, but who will never wake up to the full joy of living? Let's take some time now to reflect on our own experiences of illness and healing—not only physically but also psychologically and spiritually—and note them briefly on our third page.

Spiritual experiences have undoubtedly occurred in each person's life in the peak experiences, in the conversion from one way of living to another, and in the healing. Thus we know now that our task is not to become spiritual people or to find out what it means to be spiritual. Rather our work is much easier. We have only to discover the spiritual moments in our life and allow them more power to transform us. We are already spiritual; but we need to know those times as times of the spirit and to exploit them more effectively than we have done. Once we have located them, we can enable them to develop. They may take on a greater role in our life, making our life richer and tastier.

In the rest of this book, we'll be exploring ways to uncover the spiritual moments and allow them to blossom. And we shall develop some techniques for cultivating our spiritual experiences. Imagine coming upon a plot of land that would be nice to turn into a garden. The land, if you look closely, already contains many of the plants you want to grow in this garden. But right now they are simply growing wild, and many are not growing well because no one cares for them.

We might begin our gardening in two ways. One way would be to plow under the old growth and start with new seeds. But wouldn't it be more economical to take what is already growing there and provide some structure and care? We could remove the weeds and transplant some of the plants so that they grow with some kind of overall order. It is this second image of the garden that we will develop in this book. No radical plowing is really needed: we are already spiritual people. All we need now is some concern and care so that the spirituality we already enjoy might grow more vital and beautiful and enable us to provide meaning for our life.

How to Use This Book

Since this is meant to be a workbook and a rather personal guide on the spiritual journey, it has unusual directions for its reading. You could read it just as you would any other book, in order to gain information. But that approach would miss the real purpose for which this book was written. The exercises form the heart of the book. The rest of the text is meant as a dialogue between your experience of the work and my own. Since it takes time to do the exercises and to enter into these various experiences, my hope is that you will have this book at hand for a long time, not to be reading constantly but to return to again and again. Further, this is a beginning book from which to set forth. So it has a bibliography of books I can personally recommend. Each chapter of this book can only begin to deal with the contents. If your interest is aroused, you'll want to investigate further in the books mentioned in the bibliography. It's likely that from time to time you will be laying aside this book in order to pursue a certain matter in more depth elsewhere. And when you're done there, you can return here to enter upon a new experience.

We are all at a different stage along our journey of spiritual development, and we have various skills and interests as well. Thus this is a book from which to pick and choose as you create your own journey. Which chapters fascinate you right now? Well, go ahead and plunge into them if you like. Leave the less interesting chapters for later.

Or you may wish to follow the book's own order, for there is reason for its being so laid out. Part One contains advice for developing good prayer habits—guidelines in our prayer work to keep us from becoming bogged down or failing. It would be very helpful just to skim over these pages before going on, even if you don't want to give them much time right now by doing the exercises there. Later in your work, if you notice you're having some difficulty, you can go back to the guidelines for help.

Part Two deals with prayer exercises. Here we talk about and practice cultivating the different parts of ourselves that can be involved in prayer. In this section, the emphasis is upon development and practice. And there is a reason for our progression from mind to body to spirit. We take up the mind first because it is the most recalcitrant part of our being in terms of spiritual work. But it is also the place where we are most able to begin because of the emphasis our society places upon intellect. Then we move on to the body because it provides a very different and refreshing experience in contrast to mental work. And body work is very rewarding as well, since we usually experience quick progress and measurable results. We leave the work of the spirit until last because, being the highest form of the spiritual journey, it is the most subtle. The hope is that our work on mind and body will provide the groundwork and sharpen our perception so that we can appreciate and understand the special work of the spirit when we come to it.

Each part of this second section's practice flows naturally into a full experience of prayer, which is described in Part Three of the book. Our practice of mental prayer leads to the experiences of art and music as prayer as well as to other experiences; the practice of body awareness leads into the prayer experience of sports, dance, and the nature walk; and the practice of cultivation of the spirit leads to the prayer experiences involving story and person. So you may wish to break up the second and third sections, moving from the exercise in Part Two to the corresponding prayer experiences in Part Three. You must be your own judge of where you will begin, what you will take up, and how far you will go. The journey is above all your own. May this guide be of some use on that special unique adventure you undertake.

Two

The Pleasure Principle:
Enjoy Your Prayer

If the most difficult aspect of prayer is to begin, the next most difficult task is to continue praying. At first the novelty of prayer provides enough energy to keep us faithful. But when the novelty wears off, we need to find other means to maintain interest and commitment. How can we hope to make our lives prayerful if prayer is for us a drudge, a chore, a duty.

When I was about five years old, my mother decided it was time for piano lessons. There had always been a piano in the house, and I would climb up on the stool and bang away at the ivories from the time I first learned to crawl. Why not channel all of that banging energy into piano playing, thought my mother. So off to piano lessons I went. At first I was fascinated by the world of music as I learned how to decipher the squiggles and dots into musical sounds. And my music books were fun, for they talked not about the bass and treble clefs, but rather about a story of Papa, Momma, and Baby bears. It was more fun locating Papa bear on the piano than finding low C in the bass clef. I learned music because it was interesting.

And as I grew up, something happened to me that was both good and bad. First, my parents never forced me to practice. This laxity on their part probably contributed to my lack of discipline now. On the other hand, I never had bad childhood experiences in music. There were no sunny afternoons when I had to practice and miss out on the neighborhood ball game.

And since I played the piano only when I wanted to, all my playing was strictly for pleasure. I grew to enjoy music, and I probably played more piano than many children who were forced to practice.

The only difficulty came from my teacher's frustration. I learned what I enjoyed while the scales, exercises, and assigned pieces languished for weeks before being learned. This is one reason why I am not a concert pianist today, but also a reason why music is one of the most important parts of my life.

I played the piano so much because it was fun. Can we similarly develop a good and long prayer experience by consciously and purposely ensuring that it will be pleasurable?

The Experience of Saints

Our childhood experiences of prayer are seldom associated with fun and pleasure. Prayers were boring formalities to be endured before we could enjoy our meals or go to bed. And perhaps Sunday mornings were ruined because we were dragged off to a big church where some grown-up talked on forever.

Is it any wonder, unless we happen to be well disciplined, that we never continued praying on our own after the parental authority was relaxed? Or perhaps today we still pray in the same way. But maybe now we pray for the good of the children. After all, we think, that is the way I grew up, and it did me no harm. So now we provide the same experience for our children.

With this negative experience and attitude, what do we think about those men and women whose lives were filled with prayer? Can we really believe they were so weird as to waste precious time in the same useless activity we know as prayer? But the saints loved to pray. Often it was their favorite pastime. Assuming they were really not too different from the rest of us, they must have had a very different experience with prayer from our own.

The saints believed that prayer was enjoyable. Here is a clue that may lead us to discover true prayer. Let's look for prayer that is fun and pleasant. And if a prayer experience should be boring or downright miserable, then let's admit it and discard that prayer experience for the moment.

I don't want to imply that prayer must always be a filled-with-joy experience. Acquaintance with the mystics reveals times when the springs of joy dry up and disappear. Prayer then becomes frustrating and unrewarding. John of the Cross calls this the "dark night of the soul." But such times do not occur at the beginning of the prayer journey. The person must have already made significant progress along the way before she or he is ready to face such tests. Then such a period of dryness and aridity serves as a valuable process of growth along the path of the spirit.

But we are still at the very beginning of our journey. We are not convinced that prayer is worth our time and effort. We need to experience the fun and pleasure of prayer. So we can and should look for joy and amusement in our prayer life. Aridity and its trials will come if and when we are ready for them. That far-off time is not our concern now.

Without totally endorsing Freud's pleasure principle as the sole motivation for human behavior, we can see that much of our activity is ultimately directed toward pleasure of some kind. We could even say that the index of maturity is found in a person's ability to work at nonpleasurable tasks in order to gain a distant or delayed pleasure. A child will only work at something if the reward is immediate. An adult will be willing to work at even a distasteful task for a pleasurable reward that might not materialize for a long time.

In our prayer experience, if we are beginners, then we are like children. We will need immediate rewards that encourage us to continue our work. The big rewards of a prayerful life such as the vision of God, supreme happiness, or even a well-integrated life are a long way off and nebulous enough to have insufficient pull to draw us through the foothills of prayer.

Inertia

The old deadly sin of sloth, indolence, or just plain laziness provides one of the most difficult battles we shall have to join on our spiritual journey. We are traveling upon a road that must be walked; walking is work, and hard work at that. Where will we get the energy to do this work? And more important, how will we overcome the inertia that coaxes us to give up the journey?

The realm of prayer holds no magic. It's ironic that in the very area that people believe is filled with magic and ignorance about the way things really are, we're confronted with a lack of magic and often for the first time in our life are forced to look at reality without rose-colored glasses.

We begin with all kinds of enthusiasm and lofty ideals. We are somewhat proud of ourselves (and with justification), for we have succeeded in making a beginning in prayer. We are on our way. Just give us the next exercise, the next step, and we'll be off and running.

But shortly, perhaps just around the next bend, we run out of steam. We have no energy left. Most of us won't even finish this book before we bottom out of the experiment. Suddenly we will find a million excuses: "I don't have the time right now." "Oh, let it go for today. I'll feel more motivated tomorrow." "I'm not really making any progress. There's such a long way to go, and I'm not even moving. It's just impossible. Maybe the spiritual life is just not my bag." And if we listen to the voices of these demented monkeys within us, we'll give up and the journey will never be completed. My viewpoint may sound pessimistic, but let's be honest. The earth is smeared with aborted spiritual journeys.

We might solve this problem of no steam by finding a guru, a teacher, or a spiritual director. This person will keep us honest about our work and even order us to continue when the journey becomes monotonous. The teacher can inspire us, offer encouragement when we despair of progress, and call us to our work with the voice of authority whenever we betray our best and highest instincts through laziness or self-pity. Indeed, if we want to embark with any real seriousness upon one of the traditional paths of spirituality such as Yoga or Zen, the teacher will be vital at some point in order to keep us committed to our work and to guard against self-delusion.

But if you do not have a teacher, are you necessarily doomed from the start? True, it is rather difficult to choose one of the more disciplined paths with any real hope of success totally on your own. But the established spiritualities are not the only roads upon which the journey can be made.

Looking back at childhood, we can see two ways in which we managed to accomplish difficult tasks. First, we did our schoolwork because if we didn't, we would have to answer to our teachers and parents. We worked to avoid disapproval and punishment.

But there were other motivating factors that could galvanize our energies. We worked for rewards and for things we wanted. And our parents knew they could capitalize on this energy to encourage us to perform tasks they saw as important for us. It was relatively easy to convince me to be a good little boy, the closer Christmas came.

In the eighth grade, when my capitalistic interests were nicely developed, my mother promised me a hundred dollars if I could win a certain scholastic award. All my energies went into that work, and my winning was duly rewarded. At the time, I considered the contract a fair exchange: my mother wanted the medal; I wanted the money. Later I could see that her interest was for me and my benefit rather than for herself. She simply knew that my head was not yet mature enough to appreciate the medal for its own sake. So she added to the medal a reward that I could strive for.

Toward Self-Motivation

As children, we need motivation by outside forces to accomplish some tasks that are in our own self-interest. A mature adult, on the other hand, is self-motivating. We work because of the rewards that come from the work itself. By such a definition, few of us are fully mature adults, your author included. And we're especially infantile in the realm of prayer. Yet, paradoxically, we need not despair of prayer even though we're too childish to be up to the task. Prayer, more than any other work in our life, enables us to become self-motivating adults. One primary task of our prayer life will be growth in self-motivation.

We should think of ourselves as both child and parent in regard to our prayer life. As a parent, we have set ourselves the work of prayer, but the child will have to do the actual work. So we should make the work as appealing and pleasurable as possible. There are thousands of kinds of prayer. A child's interest soon runs out. So the parent must keep the child as interested as possible. When the child in us tires of one kind of prayer, turn his or her attention to another. The essential work in all prayer is the same—that of awakening from sleep, of coming alive to life. And although the discipline of following one narrow road of prayer has benefits, our flitting from one pleasure to another should also carry us far along our journey until we are mature enough to accept for ourselves the discipline of one path.

Distractions

But the pleasure principle will not always be easy to apply. For do we really know what true pleasure is? Unfortunately, we can mistake distraction for pleasure. But distraction is never a valid kind of prayer experience. By distraction I don't mean the little annoyances that crop up during a meditation. Distractions are enticements away from the work at hand under the pretext of offering pleasure. Indeed, if prayer is a coming awake to the reality of the world, then distraction that means losing sight of what is truly important is actually the opposite of prayer. True pleasure leads us toward the real; distraction leads us away. Pleasure places us in the midst of the present moment and at the center of our life. And it allows us to savor and enjoy that moment to the full. Distraction tries to seduce us away from the present into a false past or illusive future. It offers us a very pale imitation of joy.

Before we can hope to apply the pleasure principle in our prayer life, we must be able to distinguish between pleasure and distraction. That task will be helped by our prayer exercise for the coming week.

Scheduling a Time to Pray

Make a contract with yourself right now to spend some time each day during the next week simply enjoying yourself. Also spend at least one hour during the week doing nothing but enjoying yourself. Do not distract yourself with books, music, film, or friends. Just enjoy yourself doing nothing. You might decide to do nothing in a sitting position. But you might also walk about as long as your walk has no ulterior purpose such as exercise, errands, or sightseeing. You might also want to search for a place such as the beach, the mountains, or a nice park that's conducive to doing nothing. If you find such a place, then go there, but while you are there take time to be rather than to do anything.

After trying this prayer exercise, you will see just how hard it is to find true pleasure. All too often we settle for distraction. Yet distraction will never ultimately satisfy us. It will only anesthetize us and keep us from our search for true pleasure and fulfillment.

But true pleasure is a valuable goal and worth our efforts. During our prayer practice, we're obliged regularly to rededicate ourselves to this search for pleasure and fulfillment. We're hardly adult enough at this point to make our commitment once and for all. We need to remind ourselves constantly of our goal.

In my own prayer life, I begin with fervor and a sense of purpose and commitment. But when routine sets in, as it inevitably does, prayer becomes just another task to be done during the day's course. Following the natural progression, the prayer routine pretty soon comes to seem a drudge. Now it's something that doesn't make much difference, so it can easily be sacrificed in favor of some more important activity. And it becomes twice as easy to drop prayer the next day as well. Pretty soon there is no prayer routine anymore. And then I begin to notice how my life is slowly slipping back into unconsciousness, so I pull myself up and rededicate myself to prayer.

Three

The Work Principle: Be Serious

If you did the exercise toward the end of the last chapter, you discovered that simply enjoying yourself was much more difficult than you'd imagined. Distraction is easy, and entertainment is a facile way of passing time. But when we're thrown back completely upon our own devices, we find it difficult to experience pleasure and fulfillment.

The major religious traditions recognize this difficulty in human nature, and they place it at the very root of human existence. When we come to see how difficult it is to enjoy ourselves truly, we realize how out of touch we are with our own fulfillment. And it dawns on us what a great malaise we suffer. Humanity, showered as it is with all the incredible godlike talents and gifts at the pinnacle of creation, still has great difficulty simply enjoying itself.

A Fallen Life

Something is strangely out of kilter in our makeup. Why can't we take pleasure in the simple act of being alive? Christians speak of this estranged existence as fallen. The Buddhists label this experience *samsara;* from the experience of samsara arises the first noble truth that the world—all of existence—is suffering.

Suffering does not mean that the world is full of pain. Suffering means rather that no matter how pleasurable and satisfactory anything in our life is, it still falls short and lacks wholeness. It is not sufficient.

Buddhism proposes a path by which we might extricate ourselves from this unsatisfactory existence. Christianity proposes a way by which we can leave behind fallen existence and fulfill our original desire for wholeness.

I have come to some knowledge of this ill ease in my own life. I fill my life with various tasks. I overcommit myself, but even in my over-commitment, I feel pangs of guilt because I have a picture of myself as lazy. And when I am in the midst of my overscheduled life, I look with longing for a time of leisure, when I can exit from this rat race, when I can relax and simply be myself. I long to be alone and do some of the things I love most—listen to opera or read a book. So I block out on my schedule an evening a couple of weeks away when I will relax alone. That evening will be given over to music or a book.

And when that special evening comes, I go to my room and am im-mediately confronted with a problem. Which opera do I want to listen to, which book interests me? So I flit from choice to choice, over-whelmed by the possibilities. As the frustration builds, I consider what I could be doing tonight if I were not steeped in indecision. Then I feel guilty because there is work waiting to be done. My rest-lessness builds and builds until I rush out of the room and go for a walk.

I usually end up at the local bookstore where I browse through hundreds of books that I might buy, even though I know that in all probability I will never read them. And so the night slips by. Rather than being restored and renewed, I have spent myself escaping from the burden of leisure that I had desired so much. What happened? Why couldn't I accept this evening and spend it pleasurably with one specific activity?

We seek pleasure and enjoyment. But when we turn ourselves to-ward them, they spoil before us. And we're left with the fraudulent pleasures of distraction and the passive pleasures of being entertained. Are we so lacking and imperfect that we can't comfortably remain with ourselves in silence and enjoy the pleasure of our own company?

Pleasure Needs Working On

Although we're searching for pleasure (according to our first princi-ple), we must, paradoxically, achieve this ability to take pleasure in ourselves only by very serious and hard work. We're so estranged and cut off from fulfillment, from what we believe should come naturally to us, that we must expend considerable effort to acquire, taste, and savor what we imagine is our birthright.

The Christian myth of the Fall is so penetrating in its analysis, not because there actually was a historical Fall, but because the myth postulates a time when it was natural for humanity to be happy and self-fulfilling. We look toward this pleasure, this ease, this leisure, this fulfillment as something we should possess by nature. Yet as we move to take possession of our birthright, we find ourselves woefully cut off from it. We have lost what we believe belonged to us somewhere along the line. Thus the Christian myth posits a time, a far-off once upon a time, when we enjoyed this capacity. We have tasted it, but now we have lost it.

Cultivating the capacity for enjoyment is a great task. It will take time; it cannot be hurried or rushed. We can't accomplish it in a week, a year, or perhaps even a lifetime. To accomplish this work, we will need patience and openness. The spiritual work is not gross; its results will not be obvious to us. The rhythms of the spiritual life are very still and subtle inner movements. We have not yet so finely tuned our perceptions that we can see and discern these workings. So we commit ourselves to the path, we have faith in the path, we are patient with the path, and we are open to whatever happens to us along the path.

Let's accept as a principle that whatever happens to us is a part of the path. We won't become discouraged in our work or feel that we have taken a wrong turn. Discouragements will only make our work that much more difficult. We're on our way, and as long as we're open we're making progress.

Creating a Schedule

Since any work is difficult (and in time becomes routine and filled with drudgery), it requires discipline for its success. A prayer schedule provides us with that needed discipline. An external contract keeps us honest, prods us on over the rough places, and prevents us from falling by the wayside.

Our contract will detail just how we want to engage in this work. How much time do we actually want to set aside out of our day for meditation and prayer? There is of course no ideal schedule for everyone; we must develop our own personal schedule. But we can follow a few basic principles in negotiating our contract.

First, let's start small. Enthusiasm is normal at the beginning of the prayer work, and our initial zeal may inspire us to carve out a huge schedule, such as an hour's meditation every day. But enthusiasm is not a reliable guide. We still live in a real world that is not about to give up its demands upon us just because we want to pray. And the work of prayer, in spite of our initial enthusiasm, is difficult to justify in the face of more worldly demands and activities. Sobriety and honesty should be our watchwords. Let's err on the side of too little rather than too much. Too large a goal creates frustration. And then, disappointed in ourselves, we give up the prayer because it accuses us of our failings and lack of discipline. But if we begin with a small commitment that we can handle, we'll be able to expand it later and acknowledge our progress.

Second, we should draw up our schedule not for what we think we should be doing but rather to describe what we actually want to do now. Perhaps we believe we should meditate twenty minutes twice a day—an excellent meditation schedule. But if we're not really eager and ready to meditate forty minutes a day, it does no good to set up a schedule that will accuse us of failure and turn our prayer into a guilt-filled occasion of misery, driving us further from our sought-after pleasure. Take the time to ask yourself what you are truly eager to undertake right now. And examine your eagerness closely: is it just of this moment (the problem of enthusiasm again), or is it something I am truly ready to do? Today I may feel like meditating for an hour. Fine. But will I feel that way every day for the next four weeks?

We should have a schedule that is easily kept. Thus it should be a minimum contract. At the start of our work, we don't need additional guilt or burdens. Once we're into the work and have experienced its benefits, we'll be able to assume greater commitments and responsibilities joyfully and with full knowledge of what we're getting into. Right now we're still searching for a basic commitment to the work. We feel called to it; we want to do it. But we haven't yet experienced how we'll feel once we're into it. We're like people who do not know whether they can swim. So it's foolhardy to jump off the diving board into the depths. We may drown. But by wading out, we may test the water and our reaction to it. Our first goal is pleasure, enjoyment, and some minimal satisfaction from the work. That is enough for now.

Once we've decided how much time we wish to devote to the work, we can look over our daily routine, selecting those times when we will be both free and open to do this work well. We want times when we won't be overtired and won't be too excited to quiet down. The times must also be beneficial to us: if we're not at our peak in the morning, we probably shouldn't meditate then, at least at the outset. There is no objectively bad time. Pick a time when you're open and receptive, when you can relax without the likelihood of disturbance. The only times we'll definitely want to avoid are after a heavy meal or after a vigorous physical workout. We want a time when we're by nature quiet, not weighed down by food, concerns, or exhaustion. Then we can be open to our experience.

Let's also promise ourselves that if we run into problems, we'll renegotiate the contract rather than abandon the work. This is only a tentative schedule. We're not quite sure of ourselves at this stage. We don't know for certain how long we want to meditate. We're not positive what are the best times for our meditation. The schedule is part of our prayer experiment. We may have to change it many times before we come upon a style good for us.

The creation of this schedule is not just a prelude to prayer: it is part of the prayer experience. Through its use, we come to know ourselves better. So if after a few days we find difficulty, it is time to reevaluate. And this is not starting over, but rather a further step along the way. All previous schedules are not failures; if we were receptive, each has taught us something.

And let's be quicker to modify downward in accordance with our pleasure principle than to increase our prayer time. Expand the schedule only when you're sure you're ready and can take it without strain. But decrease it whenever the prayer itself becomes threatened with extinction. Better to pray for five minutes a day regularly than to set a schedule of an hour a day and be able to meet that schedule only one day a week.

And be mindful also of our need for a time off from prayer. True, it is best to pray every day. But we want a realistic rather than an ideal schedule. At least here at the beginning, you might want to give yourself a day or so off each week. Or you might find as you enter into the routine that you need such time off. Reschedule it into your contract instead of feeling guilty about missing a day.

Finally, we want to check ourselves from time to time. We don't want this schedule hanging over our heads. We're not absolutely accountable to it. Any life will have lapses. The schedule should never become a burden or a source of guilt. But we will want to return to our agreement regularly for evaluation of our prayer life. At those times, we may want to revise it in the light of our experience.

When we come to evaluate ourselves, we must make a distinction between abuse and accommodation. If we have failed to live up to the contract, we should not automatically decrease it. We want rather to explore whether the schedule is realistic for our life and our real desire to pray now. If we've fallen off and decide that it is mere laziness, then we will want to recommit ourselves to the original contract.

We're at war with our laziness, but we don't want to overextend ourselves either.

The Prayer Contract

Right now take pencil and loose-leaf paper and draw up a contract with yourself. Keep in mind our guidelines:

1. Start small
2. Determine what you really want to do
3. Settle upon a comfortable minimum that stretches you just a little
4. Pick the best times of day for yourself
5. When the contract is drawn up, go over it again and ask whether you really want to commit yourself to it
6. Reevaluate regularly (about once a month)

Keep this contract, and later we shall place it in the journal

Four

The Experimental Principle: Be Open

Since there are many different types of people, it follows that there are various ways we can pray. How can we expect a rather reserved person who does not enjoy emotional situations but prefers to approach the world through his or her intellect and reasoning powers to use and enjoy exactly the same prayer techniques as the person who is very open and free with his emotions but who really cannot enjoy or appreciate the subtle arguments of the philosophers? If prayer is at least as basic a part of life as eating, we can hope for as great a variety of nourishment for our spirit as we have cultivated for our bodies.

Let's extend the metaphor of food further. What if, when we were growing up, our parents had allowed us to eat only the food with which we were familiar? Children are hopelessly narrow about their likes and dislikes in food. In one period of my childhood, I preferred nothing but peanut butter and jelly. Then this staple gave way to tuna fish, followed by hot dogs, which were succeeded by a graduation of sorts to the hamburger—the American teen-ager's daily bread.

As children, we thought we had found the food we liked. We were willing to abide with it forever, or at least until our taste buds numbed at the thought of more of the same. But if our parents took their role seriously, our food horizons were forcible expanded.

"But I don't like asparagus!"

"How do you know? Have you ever tried it?"

"No, but it looks and smells funny. I don't want to eat long green sticks."

"All I want you to do is try some so that you can say you don't like it, and you'll know what you're talking about."

And when we tried it, usually with the threat of no dessert unless we did, sometimes we were surprised and this new, funny-looking, different-tasting food became one of our favorites.

We are like children when we come to prayer. Perhaps we have one prayer form we like to cling to, ignoring the many other varieties. But how can we know that these other peculiar and exotic forms of prayer are not for us? After all, we have not had sufficient experience to form any standards of taste for ourselves. Nor do we know ourselves well enough spiritually to realize the best methods of prayer for our lives. So at this beginning stage, let's not shut off prematurely any of the various techniques of prayer and spirituality. Let's regard your prayer as an adventure. We can afford to be daring, for we've nothing to lose but our inadequate preconceptions.

We're engaged upon exploration and discovery. We're seeking to find not only a way to pray but also a better understanding of ourselves and our world. Flexibility will be one of the keys to our success. We should not form at the beginning too strict an idea about prayer or about ourselves, our likes, and our dislikes. Rather let us test out various prayer styles as we go along. Gradually, as we discover more about ourselves and the experience of praying, we will be able to form a more mature judgment about the kind of prayer life that will both comfort and challenge us. Only then will the moment be right to select from the number of techniques we have experimented with the ones that proved more beneficial.

A Time to Decide

And indeed there will come a time when our searching and sampling must come to an end if we're to make further progress. One of the sad sights today is that of people running up and down the aisles of the spiritual supermarket, flitting from one fad to another as they seek to penetrate beneath the surface of life. These pilgrims go from TM to Gestalt therapy to Biofeedback to Rolfing to California Buddhism and so on. And what do they accomplish? Nothing, because they give no approach a chance to take root, without which a technique cannot bring about the great transformations they seek.

At the beginning, a variety of styles introduces us to the great scope of the spiritual journey. But a time comes when each of us must choose among the different paths. Then we'll have to put aside the other techniques and concentrate upon one way of prayer so that we know it intimately. Then it will send deep roots into our life, and we in turn will grow and change.

And let's not deceive ourselves. We'll find no form of prayer totally compatible. Our goal is not to find a prayer that is very attractive and easy. Our goal rather is to find a prayer that suits us and can help us grow. When we have decided upon such a prayer style, and when we are in a position to choose freely rather than merely accept the first spirituality that comes along, then we must be ready to make a real commitment. We have to be ready to work with it no matter what happens. We'll have to bear with it through boredom and through fears that we have chosen wrongly and through despair that we shall ever make any progress. For only with this total commitment, fidelity, and willingness to work hard will we eventually come to know ourselves and feel at one with ourselves and our world.

We don't seek new thrilling experiences or new highs each time we pray. We seek to know ourselves and to learn to see the world in a new way. These goals are not easy. We play all sorts of games with ourselves, and we see only what we think we see rather than what is really there to be seen. Only by dying to the way we are now, the way we think now, and the way we see now can we be reborn as praying people.

But any such marriage to a prayer form is still far off in our lives. Right now we're in that wonderful season of dating. Now is the time to savor and discover all the exciting possibilities of spirituality available. And as we court these various prayer forms and styles, we'll learn a little about ourselves—what appeals to us, where we're weak, ways of prayer that we can't relate to or enjoy, and, above all, experiences that make our time of prayer seem all too short.

A Meditation on the Breath

During the next week, let's sample some of the diversity of prayer forms by practicing two very different types of meditation. The first focuses upon a form; the second is actually focused upon no form at all. Our first meditation is powerfully developed in the Zen tradition. It is called meditation on the breath.

Meditation Posture and Meditation on the Breath

This and the next meditation should take about twenty minutes each to complete. However, if you think that's too much for you right now, try ten minutes. Alternate these two exercises, doing each every other day for the next week.

First take a meditation posture. All that is essential to such a posture is the alignment of your head, neck, and back in a straight line while you're in a comfortable sitting position. You may sit in a straight-backed chair or assume a cross-legged or kneeling position on the floor. It's best for the meditation, however, that you not lean your back against the back of the chair or a wall: keep your back straight by using your own muscles rather than by relying upon external supports.

This posture helps achieve the meditation state, which is midway between total relaxation and total alertness. So you shouldn't lie down; in that position, relaxation almost inevitably will dominate over alertness. On the other hand, if you take some very demanding, difficult-to-maintain posture, you'll be very alert but hardly relaxed.

Having assumed the proper sitting posture, you can turn your attention to your breathing. Simply observe your breath as it comes into and leaves your body. Don't try to change it; it will do no good to exaggerate. You want to be a very interested but uninvolved witness to your own breathing.

After you have passed a few minutes observing your breath, you may then begin to count the breaths silently. Count *one* on the inhalation and think *and* on the exhalation. Continue counting this way up to four breaths; then begin again with one. Continue this counting in series of four breaths for the duration of the meditation.

The problem of timing in meditation can be handled various ways. I myself place my watch in front of me during meditation. I can glance at it occasionally to see how much time has elapsed. You might use a small food timer with a bell. This allows you to meditate without breaking the mood.

There are two reasons for restricting the series to four. First, the object of the meditation is not to see how many breaths you can count. Counting four hundred breaths is not necessarily a sign of a better meditation than counting three hundred breaths. The object of this meditation is to be attentive to the breathing, observing it closely and allowing the breath to occupy your mind completely during the meditation. Thus our second reason: limiting the count to four makes concentration as simple as possible. You need not worry about the number you have just counted or what number comes next. Any of us could count to four even while dead drunk; it involves no great intellectual effort. Thus the mind can be fully occupied with the breath rather than with the counting. And if you should miss or forget your count, you merely start over with *one*. The counting is merely a help toward focusing more upon the breath.

While performing this meditation, remember the principles of prayer we have adopted so far. First, enjoy your meditation. In this kind of exercise, our enjoyment should focus upon the breathing. The lowly activity of breathing enables us to live. Take time now to appreciate breathing just as you might appreciate and savor a good meal. Feel the air as it comes into your nostrils and enters your lungs. Observe the path of the air in and out of your body. Enjoy each breath as if it were the last you would ever take. Think how much you would appreciate that final breath, and come to be grateful for this present breath.

Next, be serious about your meditation. Even though it is enjoyable, meditation is also work, and as you progress in your practice, you will soon discover just how difficult it can be. Now is not the time for daydreaming or thinking about other things. Now is the time to count the breath. The only way you can meditate is to learn to relax and pay attention at the same time. When you find your mind wandering, don't become angry, but be firm nevertheless. Return the mind gently to the meditation again and again as soon as you discover it has wandered off. Coax it, and be gentle when it slips away. But be firm with the monkey that lives and cavorts in your head. After all, you only want it to be quiet for ten or twenty minutes; then it can go back to its normal ways. Twenty minutes of quiet is not too much to ask even from a small child.

Meditation on the Attention

While doing the previous breathing meditation, you undoubtedly noticed your mind constantly wandering off in every possible direction. You have probably been made aware of thoughts that never would have surfaced during the course of the day because they are so trivial and peripheral to your ordinary business. Yet when we take the time to calm our mind and slow down our thoughts, all these trivial and irrelevant distractions come flooding into consciousness. It is important that we not become discouraged. Sometimes it will seem that we spend the entire meditation telling our mind to begin again after it has run off to play with some other fascination or obsession.

Another type of meditation actually uses our distractions as the object upon which we meditate. After all, if the mind is going to distract us continually from concentration upon our breathing by acting like a monkey, then let us trick the monkey by using it as our meditation object.

This meditation, like the previous one, should take from ten to twenty minutes, whatever you feel comfortable giving it. To begin, take one of the postures described in the previous meditation, making sure that your head and back form a straight line. Imagine a string attached to the top of your head. As the string is pulled, your body straightens up. Again, the secret to any meditation posture is that you are both relaxed (you cannot meditate if you are tense) and at the same time alert (you cannot meditate if you are asleep).

Now close your eyes and observe your thoughts. But detach yourself from the thoughts; don't allow them to catch you up so that you become involved in them. Rather be like a person sitting by a river. You sit and watch. Soon logs come into your vision. The logs are floating down the river. You don't follow them; you let them float by. While they're before you, you observe them. But you don't try to stop them. You don't swim out to them and climb on board. You don't try to follow them downstream. You are not your thoughts in this meditation. Rather, you are the observer watching thoughts come into and vanish from consciousness.

Over the next week or so, experiment with these two kinds of meditation. Give each one a real chance before you decide that one is better for you. In the supermarket of spirituality, it does no harm to try out many different styles of prayer before making a purchase. Be open to the many ways and paths. The time for a choice and commitment to one will come later.

Five

The Imaginative Principle: Be Original

We in the West are not accustomed to regarding prayer under the aegis of imagination. Our model for prayer life has been conformity rather than originality, and this limitation has been partly to blame for the death of prayer in the West. Prayer was often used as a way in which the believer could mold himself or herself onto the pattern of divinity. Such a view comes out most strongly in the most popular inspirational book in Christianity, *The Imitation of Christ*.

Granted that one of the main objectives of the spiritual journey is to unfold the divine potential within the human being: prayer can be seen as a conforming unto the godhead. But why not model ourselves more on the living God than upon God the divine Lawmaker. Creator is a central description of the deity in Judeo-Christian tradition. If we wish to mold ourselves after the divine principle, what better way to become like Him than to join in His self-expression, through the creation of the world in the power of love. And we can express ourselves through our own loving creations, whatever they may be. As we journey through this book, we'll discover that most experiences in prayer are experiences of creation—creation of music and art, creation through movement, creation of stories, and ultimately the creation of ourselves as human beings in community with others. To come fully alive to our potential is the true path of prayer. And our imaginative expression of ourselves can open up for us infinite possibilities of personal growth and development.

Our prayer work, then, will be a work of increasing, exercising, and developing our imaginations. Unfortunately, many of us have allowed ourselves to be routinized. Our imaginations have been dulled if not totally put to sleep. We all too readily allow others the work of imagining for us. We live in a media-saturated society. And inundated with stimuli, we're not compelled to call upon our own imaginations. The mere flick of the television knob allows us to be fed by the imagination of others. We become passive rather than creative.

The Poverty of Pornography

Consider the example of music. Until our generation, music depended to a great extent upon amateurs such as ourselves who had grown up taking music lessons as a part of our adolescence. Our life was filled with music because we either played ourselves or lived with someone who did. Concerts were special events, when we could be exposed to great music professionally played. But today our lives are saturated with music through the ever-present stereo. Everyone who wants to has heard Beethoven's Fifth Symphony more times than even symphony orchestra members would have heard it in the old days. Fifty years ago, it was impossible for a music lover to become bored by the Fifth. Today each new recording, unless it is a totally new revelation, is greeted by the record reviewer with a groan.

And our modern stereo leaves little to the imagination. The performance is flawless, the sound nearly perfect. Many people prefer recorded sound to the live experience. As an addicted music lover, I do not bemoan this development. But my enjoyment of music depends much less upon my imagination today than it would have fifty years ago, when I might have heard a live performance of the Fifth five times in my life. The rest of my acquaintance with that masterpiece would have come through a piano transcription, which I would play to the best of my ability while I left my imagination to fill in the orchestration and to make up for my technical inadequacies.

Philip Roth once argued against pornography, not because it is bad in itself or because it is obscene or because it perverts little children, but because it dulls our own imagination. And the erotic is one form of imagination that almost every human being shares. Pornography supplants our own creative erotic fantasies with some mass-produced version usually written, not to stimulate primarily, but rather to make money. And as Roth points out, the mass product is often not on the same creative level as our own fantasies could be if they were allowed to mature and develop. Pornography becomes a substitute for imagination. And our media are pornographic in the same sense—not because they are erotic, but because they rob us of the chance to develop our own creative powers.

33

A Challenge to See

Imagination is the gift of being able to consider the possibilities. In our prayer life, we should therefore be imaginative, avoiding the routine and the ruts into which we so easily allow ourselves to fall. There is no question but that the work of prayer includes much dullness and boredom. But if we give in to that dullness and routine, if we stop searching for the unique, totally original gift of the present moment, then our meditation dies. In meditation we practice being alive to the inherent possibilities of each moment, and such practice draws upon our imagination for its success.

Imagination provokes us into risking. It tempts us to do things we have never done before. It dares us risk what we consider ourselves incapable of doing. I myself, for example, have very little visual artistic ability. I can't draw a straight line with a ruler. But why can't I in my prayer work allow myself the luxury of drawing? Is there some heavenly rule etched upon the firmament to the effect that Dick Chilson shall never draw? No. But I have lived my life as though there were such a rule, and I have been the poorer for it. In my prayer, I am offered a laboratory where I may experiment with myself. Perhaps I do have artistic talents. But I will never know unless I allow myself the luxury of experimentation and failure. People who think they know themselves and their capabilities are actually very unimaginative. The imaginative people do not know themselves; they consider themselves and their capabilities a hidden treasure that they can explore for the rest of their lives. Thus they are always growing and interesting.

Our development need not stop until our death—if then. And if our development does stop—if we ever believe that we're fully formed and completed, with nothing else to do or explore—it is a sure sign that we're already dead. I have the hunch that work in an area where we feel impoverished offers us greater potential rewards than plowing a field where we are already expert and in complete control.

Meditation of the Thousand-Petaled Lotus

As a beginning exercise in the prayer of imagination, let us explore the meditation of the thousand-petaled lotus. It can open us to the possibilities of imagination and awaken our imaginative powers.

The lotus is a beautiful flower that seems to have an infinite number of petals surrounding its bright center. In this meditation, we begin with some core idea, word, or concept and we place it in the center of our meditation, which resembles the core at the center of the lotus. We choose a rather neutral word, at least in the beginning—a word that doesn't conjure up strong positive or negative feelings. Later, as we move deeper into the work, we can use this exercise to explore charged concepts. But right now, we want to expand the imagination rather than dig into our psyche. So let's choose some idea that we would like to pray with, expand, and explore for about twenty minutes. For our example here we will choose *red*.

In our meditation, we want to explore the associations that our core concept leads us to. Once we have put our concept into the center of our meditation, we begin constructing the thousand petals of the lotus around that center. We do this by a process of free association with the central concept. Beginning with our concept *red*, we wait until an association appears such as *color*. This becomes the first petal. We return to our central concept and wait for another association to arise. Pretty soon *fire* comes to mind. We return to the original concept and continue the meditation in this way. Each time we return to the original concept; we do not associate with the petal concepts. As we gain proficiency with this meditation, we can use it to explore and learn about many things. One day we might want to explore the notion of something such as *God* or *love* or *jealousy* or anything else we might wish to come to know in more depth.

Six

The Journal Principle: Keep a Record

As we begin this prayer journey, we encounter a real difficulty that arises out of Western skepticism concerning the spirit. For four hundred years, a major part of our culture has been in rebellion against the whole idea of the soul or the spirit. Our science has matured under the principle that what cannot be objectively verified or measured is not important or does not exist. And since we are products of such thought, we can't help but be deeply influenced by it. Perhaps you have great difficulty believing there even could be such a thing as a spirit, although by the fact that you're reading this book, you show that you're at least open to the possibility. Even if we can convince ourselves we have a spiritual dimension, our culture is so unskilled in the discernment of the spiritual reality that we will need a tool that will enable us to objectify what is happening to us on the journey. We need a tool by which we can map the movements of our spiritual development. After a few months in this work, the great danger is that we might feel we have made no progress at all, that nothing has happened.

A Yardstick to Measure By

If we take the time and the effort to keep a record of our journey, and if at the end of that few months we reexamine that record, we'll be amazed at the progress we make. But the spirit is so shimmering and intangible, so gossamer and insubstantial (in a descriptive rather than a valuative sense) that it is difficult if not impossible for us (especially at the beginning) to be aware of and appreciate its workings and movements.

This valuable tool takes the form of a journal. And I would like to suggest a possible shape for this journal. It is best to keep it in a loose-leaf notebook so that you can add paper as needed to each of the sections. In fact you already have some material to enter—the exercises you did at the start of the book. Besides the notebook and loose-leaf sheets, you'll need a set of subject dividers (at least five). Throughout the rest of the book, we will return to the journal as appropriate and amplify how it is to be used in detail. But for now, I'll explain those sections where you can begin working today and I'll only sketch in the others. If you wish to see just how the completed journal looks, you may look up the page references now instead of waiting.

On Using the Journal

You'll want to work in your journal from now on in your journey. But as with the prayer schedule, you don't want this valuable tool to become a burden. So begin gently and with a commitment to working in the journal that does not weigh you down. Allow the journal and its value to grow on you so that you work more and more in it because you've come to perceive its value rather than because you feel you have to.

In this entire work of prayer, be very careful at the outset not to overburden yourself. Allow yourself just enough experience to entice you further in the work. Rushing or overburdening yourself is unfair to your inner life. These experiences need time to develop and grow.

Life Diary

This first section is a regular diary or log of our lives. Here we enter events, feelings, and thoughts that occur to us during the day. Ideally we might want to make some entry each day. Our work with the diary can take as much or as little time as we like. There will be times in our life when our diary work will consume much time and other times when it consists of mere jottings or notes from time to time. There is no hard-and-fast rule on time here.

The first pages are your examination of life, on which you worked at the outset. Right now it is sufficient if from time to time you record here things that are happening in your life that you consider important or even just worth mentioning. But this tool will be only as valuable as the care and time that go into creating it. As you begin working in the diary, you'll grow to value it more and find yourself returning to it much more often. If you never use the diary, you can't expect it to be of any real help.

Throughout the journal, be sure to identify each entry by full date, time of entry, and place (if it differs from the usual). This information could prove very valuable in the future, and it takes practically no time to include it. As you move through periods of crisis, you may want to enter items each day so that you have a way to express your thoughts and feelings about what is happening to you. The diary can provide a forum where each of us can sort out and come to a better understanding of what is happening in her or his life. The diary, in other words, can create prayer.

Throughout the journal, the idea is not to be analytical so much as descriptive. This is not an instrument of explanation so much as a mirror in which we can see the flow of our life from period to period. Our ideal is more of a description of what is happening and how we think and feel about our life than an attempt to analyze and solve the mystery of existence.

Dream Diary

In the second section, we keep a record of all the dreams we remember. Dreams can be of enormous importance for our spiritual development. We'll discuss them later; at this point, all that is needed is that you should record each dream as fully as possible.

To record your dreams, recount them in the diary in the first person singular, present tense—I run, I see, I reach, and so on. This point of view preserves their vividness. Avoid any attempt to analyze what the dream means as you record it. If you want to analyze the dream, do so in a different part of the journal (perhaps an entry in prayer experiences, to be mentioned presently). Then if you wish in the future to consult your analysis, you can do so by matching up the dates of entry. If there is important information in your waking life that has relevance to the dream (for example, I go to an amusement park that day and then dream about amusement parks), then you should record that information in the daily diary and just note that there is a dream entry related to it in the dream diary. The dates will help you match up the different sections of the journal so that you can easily retrieve all the information. But for your work on dreams, you want the dream contents as pure as possible. Further information on dreams is found in the chapter on story (page 112).

Prayer Diary

In the third section of our journal, we will want to record our prayer schedule and each change or modification in that routine. Here we can place the contract we worked out earlier (page 25). Each time we engage in a prayer activity, we might note it in the journal. This should be a very brief log such as, "Nov. 2, 1977, 5 PM, in my room, meditated on breath for twenty minutes."

If something worth noting occurs in the meditation, you might take a sentence to note it. This section is not the place for extensive entries, however. It is really just a log of your prayer practice. Don't write more than a sentence or two here about any prayer work. You might note whether the work was enjoyable or boring on a certain day or during a certain period. You might note the cause of any restlessness or difficulty.

When you've accumulated a bank of experience, you might want to compare the prayer diary with the other diaries to discover correlations between your prayer experiences and the rest of your life. In this way, you can become better acquainted with your spirit's operation. For example, after that previous entry, you might enter the following comments after your meditation: "Feeling of calm and opening. Easy period of time."

Prayer Experience

Here we record our prayer experiences. This section will be more fully explained in Part Three of this book. Here we will record the contents of our prayer experiments and experiences—which we will encounter in Parts Two and Three of this book. The prayer diary, which was just discussed, is a record of our prayer practice; thus it is confined to short entries. But now we're considering a record of our experiences in prayer, so the entries will be longer and more fully developed. You will learn how to record each of these experiences as we discuss them throughout the book. Now I simply want to sketch in this section so that it is available to you if you wish to work in it. During your journey through this book, if you have any prayer experiences that you'd like to recount in fuller detail than called for in the prayer diary, enter them here.

Prayer Gifts

In this final section, you'll eventually gather your prayer gifts—those prayer experiences that have lasting meaning for you. You'll want to copy here favorite prayers you have either written yourself or found in your reading. Here you'll preserve stories, dreams, and other materials valuable in opening yourself to the inner world of prayer. Actually you're compiling your own personal book of prayer, which will aid you in your journey of awareness and discovery.

These are the materials that you find valuable during your journey and which you'll want to return to over and over again. This is your own book of inspiration, where all the peak experiences of your prayer life are collected and treasured. As you return to these experiences again and again in your journey, you'll find them deepening and you'll be further enriched by them. These entries usually will take a greater amount of time—about half an hour or more—than the entries in the diary sections.

If you take your time, your prayer journey will likely grow and not be aborted by an eagerness to have too much too soon. As you begin your journal, you may want to work just in the prayer diary with a few entries from time to time in the daily diary section. Then if you want to add some dreams, you can begin working there. Only later will you begin serious work in the prayer-experience section, and from your work in that section will come material for the final division of prayer gifts. But here at the beginning, regular entries in the prayer diary can reveal to you the outlines of your prayer journey and provide hints to the flow of your inner development.

By no means is the journal an end in itself. It is a tool—valuable and perhaps even necessary. But it is not itself prayer, although in the prayer-experience section, it contains the movements of your prayer, and in the prayer gifts, it will eventually hold the pathways you have found to prayer. But it is above all a means to praying, not the end itself.

II

PRAYER
EXERCISES

Seven

Cultivating Silence

There are four exercises that we shall examine in this section: silence, concentration, the body, and the spirit. But what are prayer exercises? They are analogous to the scales and studies that form a part of the practice with a musical instrument. In piano practice, an aspiring player would begin with scales and then pass on to some finger-dexterity exercises such as Hanon or Czerny. These practices accomplish two things: they warm up the fingers to play music, and they also build those skills and techniques needed for serious music. They are of course, playing the piano, and in some sense, they are musical. But they are not really music; they are not ends in themselves in the way that a piece by Chopin or Bach is. Similarly these prayer exercises are really praying, but they're not the peak experiences of prayer that we'll discuss later. They're important exercises to provide the necessary experiences and skills that enable us to pray fully.

Our first prayer exercise is the cultivation of silence. Today we recognize a need for quiet in our lives. Throughout the Christian experience, distractions—as the old terminology called them—formed the major problem in prayer. Something is always distracting us from full concentration upon the business of praying. And experience at prayer shows us that in prayer we are most vulnerable to distractions in our life: we don't notice them as much in other areas. Distractions are actually a form of noise, so we'll examine silence by first reviewing places where noise intrudes into our life.

For our purposes, noise is whatever keeps us from prayer. Prayer is an attitude and environment of silence. So noise is whatever damages or destroys our prayer. We begin our investigation by simply observing the world around us. Even in a relatively quiet room, we can still hear noise. It is a continual part of our lives. It prevents us from focusing our attention. It interrupts us with its continual presence. We're usually not aware of the noise, simply because we shut it out in order to turn our attention to more necessary matters. But when we shut out noise, we also narrow our consciousness: we're not aware of all that is going on in our environment. Narrowing your consciousness is the exact opposite movement from prayer; in prayer we open ourselves up to the environment so that we can fully experience our world.

We also normally experience the noise of different tasks and enterprises competing for our attention. The average American is tremendously overcommitted in his or her life. Our lives are filled to the brim and overflowing with all sorts of tasks, relationships, and even ways to relax and have fun. When on a certain day I'm committed to three things and have time enough for only two, I experience a form of noise. The result is that I either rush through the three or I decide to do only two, living with the nagging noise of guilt for not doing the third also. And this noise enters not through my ears, but rather in a more subtle way through another channel of my nervous system.

The media blitz is noisy. Our grandparents were not nearly as bombarded by stimulation as we are. Consider the seemingly simple act of driving down a highway. Our body, mind, eyes, and ears are engaged in driving the car. Scenes along the highway, both natural and billboard, attract our attention for a brief but powerful moment as we zoom along at fifty-five miles an hour. In the time it took Grandpa to pass a tree or a cow as he drove his wagon, we have seen forty or fifty different things that compete for our visual attention. But this is not all: it is difficult to find a car today without a radio—and usually that radio is on whenever the car is running. So auditory stimulation competes for our attention. And finally, unless we're alone, we are also engaged in conversation with our passengers (and with all the other noise to contend with, is it any wonder conversation has been corrupted from an art into drivel?). There may even be other factors, such as the gum we are chewing, calling for attention.

We are adept at manipulating all these various stimuli so that we can to some measure succeed in doing all together. But if we really consider all that is calling for our attention here in this scene, we find it to be incredibly noisy. Only by screening out 90 percent of the environment do we manage to pay attention to 10 percent at one time. But then what do we call this neglected 90 percent if not noise—unwanted but unnecessary interfering stimulation.

Far from seeing this media blitz as a nuisance, we are actually addicted to it. I go through times when the FM radio is on all the time. And never during that time do I give my full undivided attention to it. Indeed, it is playing as I write this sentence. The music forms part of my background to fill in the silence that I fear and avoid. We create noise because we're afraid of the silence, and then we become addicted to the noise.

We believe in the motto "More is better." American culture values television, where entertainment comes neatly packaged in thirty-minute segments. An evening of television will likely mean giving attention to six different programs during the course of three hours (assuming we don't channel-hop during the programs themselves). And each successful program must suck us into it during its short time and then leave us satisfied in less than half an hour. Such a barrage of entertainment is noisy.

Films have caught on to this trend. Why should the double feature be popular? It came into existence, not for artistic reasons, but for purely economic purposes. A good film is meant to be a satisfying and fulfilling experience in itself; a great film demands a certain amount of time in order to be digested and appreciated. But how can this process occur when barely ten minutes after one experience, we are plunged into another that may be as different from the first as night from day? And we as consumers fall into this trap. We consider a double feature a bargain. I'll wait until the film I want to see is on a good double feature so that I can get my money's worth—as though art were measured by the quantity rather than the quality of entertainment. More is better—we actually want to be blitzed.

Relationships cause more noise in our lives. Because we live in a

43

highly mobile society, we can actually carry on our lives in an area of about one hundred square miles. We have many more relationships and interests than people in the past, who were restricted to the area covered on foot or horseback. I can find myself running for weeks on end from one relationship and interest to another, with never any real time for silence in between. These outside noises provide areas to focus upon as we begin our quest for silence.

The Noise Goes Inside

I saw a need for silence in my own life, not because of any rules concerning the spiritual life, but because I found my life too noisy. And so I began making that silence possible through meditation. But as I entered into meditation, I discovered that the external noise was the least of my problems. That noise was easily dealt with. When we begin to seek silence so that we can meditate, the real noise makes itself heard in our meditation. Not the drilling in the street, not the Muzak in the supermarket, not the screaming of children. The real culprit is the chattering of my own busy mind.

The mind is an incredible twenty-four-hour radio, broadcasting three or four stations simultaneously. And we have become so accustomed to this barrage of noise and static that we're not even aware it's there. It is simply part of human existence. As with the radio that plays in the background while I work or read. I'm not aware of it until I attempt to turn it off and be in silence. Then I run into trouble: it won't turn off. At the beginning of our search for silence, we discover a more powerful brand of the noise we originally wanted to escape.

And once I have come to grips with the noise in my mind, once I have learned to slow down, to turn off the different stations one by one, lo and behold: instead of the desired silence, I find another kind of noise. Now my body speaks up. Unless I'm in touch with my body, I'm usually quite insensitive to its sounds.

But the body makes all kinds of noises. Most teachers advise against meditation for a couple hours after a meal. We might think that they're just being scrupulous, there is no great harm here. So we ignore the advice, and nothing disastrous happens except that we feel slightly bloated during the meditation. Yet as we enter more deeply into the silence, we begin to hear the noises our body makes after a meal. And we find that at deeper and subtler levels, our silence is being consumed along with our food. There are gurglings, motions, and waves that we feel within us when our body is filled with food.

Or we soon learn to feel our fatigue and tension when we sit down to meditate. If I'm angry when I sit to meditate, I find an incredible amount of noise, which prevents me from being silent: that noise is my anger surging up through my being. And should I attempt to push it down or ignore it, it comes flowing back once my guard is lowered. As we enter into the silence, we discover where the real noise of our lives lies: the noise of our minds and bodies. And the external noises become secondary and easy to cure.

We can deal with this new kind of noise just as we have come to terms with external noise. But it seems that the deeper we proceed into the silence, the more aware we become of different kinds of noise. For example, what of the noise of competition? Almost everything today involves competition—our jobs, education, and relationships. And when we begin to meditate and do spiritual work, we bring this sense of competition with us. When we sit to meditate, our minds are filled with all the goals and achievements we want from the meditation. I want to see God; I want to be less nervous; I want my life to be more fulfilled; in three months, I want this noise to stop. Thus we compete against another person who meditates, against some ideal of meditation, or against ourselves if there is no one better around. But eventually we discover that all of the competition, all of the expectation is really noise that disturbs the silence and hinders our progress.

Silencing the Noise

As we embark upon meditation, we also discover that noise is relative. The noise in my life depends much more upon where I am and how I feel than upon objective factors. We have all noticed how the ticking of a clock, which we were never aware of all day long, can suddenly assume a tremendous power at night and prevent us from sleeping. My perception of noise is much more dependent upon me than it is upon the noise. We can discover and expand our relativity to noise through meditation. We never judge a meditation by saying it was not as good as yesterday because there was too much noise today. Meditation's task is not some distant goal or state of bliss. It is the simple process of being open to what is there. If today we happen to be noisy, then we should be open to the noise and accept its presence.

And we should notice where we are in meditation. It is important to be aware that yesterday the meditation was quiet, but today it is filled with noise. The entries in our prayer diary will help here. Such observation opens us up to ourselves as we learn to become aware of the state of mind we're in. But we must avoid the trap of saying "Yesterday it was a good experience. Why is it so bad today?" Such an attitude is competition and noise. Instead, observe that today I must be distracted by something; today something is going on with me so that I'm not in the same mood as yesterday. But I'm now in a different mood, which I can be in and explore just as I did in yesterday's quieter mood. Such an attitude allows us to become quiet and gives us control over ourselves. Negative judgment only increases the noise that disturbed us in the first place. Acceptance and compassion upon ourselves calm and often quiet the noise.

Meditation on Noise

Paradoxically we can achieve silence through the actual use of noise. Take a soft distant sound in your present environment; choose a noise you are not aware of until now when you begin to look for it—distant traffic, rain, or voices and distant music from another room. You can meditate upon this noise and deepen your own silence. Meditation combines relaxation and attentiveness. Sitting and listening to something you can almost hear enables you to enter a meditative state. Don't strain, don't try to pick out the words. Just sit, relaxed, and listen.

But we can go even further. If you are plagued by a certain kind of noise, you can actually learn how to let that noise pass right through you so that it no longer disturbs. All it takes is practice—practice, not in the tense situation (such as at three in the morning when the noise is keeping you awake), but rather when you are relaxed and undisturbed.

The Porous Body

First let the noise strike you just as it does when it disturbs you. Then for twenty minutes see if you can imagine yourself becoming porous so that the sound no longer hits you but instead passes right through you. With successive practice sessions and imagination, you will be able to achieve this state. Then, whenever the noise is a nuisance, you can go into the meditative state and allow it to pass through you. Thus it will no longer disturb.

Again there is nothing magical. You're simply taking advantage of the fact that noise is subjective and relative.

Certain noises can sometimes actually create silence—for example, heartbeats, the sound of the seashore. Once again we see how relative

46

silence is. In fact, total silence is as bad as noise. A totally silent environment can be filled with apprehension and discomfort.

Meditation to Music

Music can help us create a silence. Find a piece of music that calms you. A quiet, slow-moving piece is best. And select a piece with a melody that does not really grab you but instead allows you to continue your own process of relaxation.

Mantra Meditation

Mantra is a Sanskrit word referring to a "word" or "sound" used in meditation. The traditional use of a mantra creates silence in meditation. Select a comforting, soothing word, preferably one that does not have an emotional charge for you. Words with soothing syllables and sounds such as r's, l's, and s's are good. You might even want to make up a nonsense word of your own.

Then sit straight, close your eyes, and say the word over to yourself aloud again and again. After a few moments, you can stop saying the word, but let its repetition continue in your mind. Be with the word in a quiet relaxed way. If it should stop and other thoughts come into your mind, that is all right. When you recognize you have drifted from the mantra, simply and gently return to it and allow it to continue. Let nothing disturb the relaxation you are creating.

Through the mantra, we put one noise in our mind as a means of shutting down the thousands of other noises that are there. It is better to have just one noise than to have fifty.

If you cannot create your own mantra, you may use words such as your first name, or try "one" or "ah." Or if you wish to be authentically Indian, you may use the traditional *Om*. At this stage of meditation, the word is not as important as the process of centering and quieting down. Only much later in the spiritual journey do the mantras themselves assume different powers.

If you have taken the mantra, you'll repeat it over and over. After a while, you'll notice that the other noises have gone away. Eventually, you'll find that even the mantra will disappear for a time, and you'll enjoy perfect silence. But you must let this process occur naturally. There is no way in which you can force it. Force will simply guarantee that the silence will never occur.

Being Silent

The best and most elementary exercise in silence involves entering into silence for at least ten minutes a day. In addition, let's agree to be silent for one period of an hour during the week. At first this idea threatened me. How would I manage to spend an hour with no distractions and with nothing to do? But once I overcame my fears and doubts, I discovered that an hour of silence is all too short.

So let's create some silence. This does not imply that we must do nothing; we could pursue some activity such as knitting or whittling. The distinction is that we are not doing *something*. The joy of whittling and knitting comes partially from the rhythm and monotony of the task, which allows a person to enter a quiet realm. These tasks involve repeating a motion again and again so that our bodies are involved in a kind of mantra. This is not the same kind of activity involved in baking a cake or repairing a car, jobs that demand our minds to be more engaged upon the work at hand. But if we are able, the best way to spend our silence is to do absolutely nothing. In the Bible, we read that God worked for six days creating the world. On the seventh day, he rested. Let us imitate him for a few minutes each day and one hour this week: this could be our Sabbath.

Eight

Cultivating Concentration

To create silence in the traditional methods of meditation, such as by the use of the mantra or concentration upon the breath, is to enter into the exercise of concentration. Our mind is very active, like a monkey constantly chattering and running all around looking for trouble. Or it is a radio playing several stations at one time. When we begin meditation, we must deal with this intractable mind. It will do everything in its power to draw notice. When we pretend not to notice it, our monkey mind will hit us, scratch us, bite us, and draw our attention back. It demands to be noticed. And as soon as we sit down in quiet, the mind will become our greatest obstacle—with its constant jabber, restlessness, and even trickiness.

Gentle but Firm

So how do we turn off our mind? How will we be able to tame the monkey? We will never tame either the mind or the monkey through the use of force. We might break it or even kill it through force, but we will never tame it. To tame our mind, we must learn to be infinitely patient with all of its caprices, but at the same time we must never give an inch on what we want. When we sit to meditate with our mantra, we suddenly find ourselves thinking about dinner, and soon we consider what will happen after dinner, and we think about the conversation we must have with the children about the bike left in the driveway. Three minutes into this reverie, we realize we are not meditating anymore.

What happens now? The normal reaction is "I failed. Here I have been sitting for ten minutes, and I haven't really been meditating. I suppose I should take ten more minutes, but I don't want to. My meditation is ruined for today. I've got to go back and start over again. I'll never get anywhere with this business."

With such an attitude, the conclusion is right: we never will get anywhere.

Instead, let's respond to our distractions as follows: "OK, little mind, you have had your fun. Now how about coming back to the mantra. You don't want to come back? Aw, come on back. You'll like it." Never grow angry or become upset with yourself. That achieves nothing.

We must avoid despairing about ourselves or our work. For instance, I must learn to deal with my anger. And if I'm in one of my angry states, the anger shoots right up my spine when I sit down to meditate. It is like a great flaming sword in the middle of my meditation. At first I said that I could not meditate when I was angry. My anger disturbed and destroyed my meditation. My response was to give up. But giving up would accomplish nothing. Instead, I could learn to look upon my anger, not as the enemy who destroys meditation, but rather with compassion as something within myself. For my anger is a part of me, and I must have compassion upon the anger, or I cannot have compassion upon myself.

Instead of fighting anger during meditation, I began to just look at it. I let it be, but I did not become involved. I separated myself from it so that I could observe it better. Here is the real trick. We are too involved and wrapped up in ourselves. And when my mind goes tripping off in meditation, I assume that it is I who am tripping off; I become upset with myself. If I can separate myself from the distraction (and this is not the same as having no interest in it at all), then I can sit here in my anger and observe it with a sense of detachment. And with distance between myself and my anger, I can learn about it—what it needs, why it is there in the first place, what it wants from me. And by having compassion or love for the anger, I can help it change. Be infinitely patient, and never give an inch.

Temptations to Give Up

About two weeks into meditation, another problem arises. The day comes when you feel just too tired or overextended to fit the meditation into your schedule. So you let the meditation go just for that day. Then the next day something else comes up, but now it is a little easier to say no to the meditation. Soon you're not meditating anymore.

Or take another instance. You have made a contract with yourself to meditate for ten minutes a day. But one day, you're distracted, and

50

yet you attempt to meditate. Five minutes into the meditation, you realize nothing is going to happen today. Your mind and body are too full of noise, so you conclude that you're wasting your time. A thousand things are on your mind, and you could be doing a thousand things in the next five minutes if you weren't sitting here wasting time.

What do we do in such a situation? Do we admit to ourselves that nothing is going to be accomplished in meditation today? Do we compromise and only sit five minutes that day? No, this is not the course of action. When we surrender like this, the score is meditation: 0, monkey mind: 1.

The mind is playing tricks on us: remember it will do anything it possibly can to stop us from the work of meditation, which threatens to tame it. And we must fight with all our wits; we're up against the one opponent fully as strong and crafty as ourselves because that opponent is ourselves. You can win this round by the following response: "OK, you're distracted today, but you're going to fulfill the contract. No matter how distracted, you're going to sit here five more minutes until you have completed your ten minutes of sitting."

If we can gain this discipline over ourselves, the mind will acknowledge who is in charge. Nor will the second five minutes be wasted, just as the first five minutes were not really in vain. In this time, we have come to see our mind, and we have begun to exert control over it—hardly a small accomplishment, even if it doesn't fulfill our ideal of what meditation should be.

If my mind can wrench me from the business of meditation just by complaining that it's not in the mood, then there will never be any progress made in the work of meditation. We are aiming toward a new hierarchy of control, where the spirit (who I truly am) controls my life and gently rules over the mind and body. Too often now, our minds and bodies tyrannize over the spirit because they are not able to rule properly; proper ruling simply is not their task.

Avoid Judgments and Criticism

There is no such thing as a bad meditation. Beginners run into this problem: they're not sure they have understood the directions correctly. They fear they are meditating wrongly. And when they sit down to meditate, their minds taunt them that they're missing the boat. After the meditation, they wonder whether they got anything out of it.

But learning to meditate is itself part of the process of meditation.

Indeed, it is truly meditation. And we *will* learn to meditate if we want to. It is a simple and natural process. Many people have learned how to meditate with no formal instructions whatever; they picked it up as part of their process of living.

When we consider the lives of creative people, we find that they have on their own discovered ways to find silence so that they might hear the still voice within. Immanuel Kant, the great philosopher, took a very precise daily walk, which included standing and staring at a certain tree for a considerable period of time. This daily routine enabled him to go deep within himself. His walk opened Kant to the creative spirit inside him and allowed his insights into the world to emerge.

And we can enter that same process. How? It is easy. Sit down and do nothing, or sit down and repeat the mantra. But observe what is happening when you sit; observe the process. And you will discover how to deal with it and how to use it correctly.

No Expectations

To meditate, we must give up our expectations. They hinder and block our progress. Our dreams of becoming saints, or seeing God, or reforming our lives—all are hindrances along our path. It is true that these expectations may have provided our motivation for meditation in the first place, but now that we are meditating, it is time to let them go. Instead, seek motivation from within the meditation itself.

Here is a time of peace and quiet when I can sit and do nothing. Here is a time when I am totally available just for myself. Don't we deserve this kind of time in our lives? This itself is reason enough for meditation.

As long as we believe we know where we should be going, we prevent ourselves from perceiving and enjoying the actual path we're traveling along. Any expectation is really a trap our mind has laid for us. With the distraction of the expectation, we're likely to miss the forest for the trees.

But as we sit each day and meditate, we'll learn slowly to give up our expectations in the same way as we learn to meditate: we learn by doing and by being observant. We will come to a point where we ourselves realize that the expectations are standing in our way, and we'll let go naturally. It is not a big deal. There is no easy way to fail in this work as long as we have good will, patience, and consciousness. The enemies are: routine, carelessness, and sleep.

Accept each meditation as a dearly loved child. We accept each for what it is, and we don't waste energy comparing it with someone else's meditation or with other meditations we ourselves have had. Like children, meditations are unique. If a certain meditation was not an experience of indescribable bliss I do not love it any the less: its own experiences, whatever they are, are unique and not to be duplicated; it offers me a gift of great value.

To paraphrase Jesus, "Sufficient unto the day is the meditation thereof." Who we are and what we experience right now is of supreme importance and worth more than all the memories of yesterday or the dreams of tomorrow. If we learn this lesson in meditation, we can apply it in actual living. Then we can move into the real quotation from Jesus: "Sufficient unto the day is the evil thereof." Don't look for tomorrow, and don't dwell in the past. Live for today—the only moment in which we can be fully alive.

Concentration Defined

Concentration is a bad word to use here, but it is traditional. We must, however, avoid the idea that it involves force or effort. It is not a process of shutting out thoughts from our consciousness. It is not deciding to sit and repeat the mantra for twenty minutes while fighting against any thought that attempts to break the meditation. Concentration is rather sitting down to be with the mantra. And it means sitting with mindfulness. If any thoughts arise, I do not attach myself to them. The trick is not to become involved. This is possible. But it is not possible to prevent the thought from arising into consciousness in the first place.

Let us return to an image we have already used (page 31)—counting logs at the river. We pretend we are sitting comfortably under a tree at the bank of a great river. As we sit quietly looking out over the peaceful river, a log comes into view. As the log passes by, we notice it but we don't become involved with it. We don't get up, jump into the river, and swim out to it so that we can climb on board. Instead, we observe the log as it floats downstream; pretty soon it is gone from view. We do, however, continue to observe the river.

When we become attached to the thoughts that arise, we're mistaking the thoughts for our mind. The mind is not the log but the river. As we continue in meditation, we shall want to begin observing the time between logs. That short space of thoughtlessness is where we can find out what we're really like. We have come to see ourselves as our thoughts, our ideas, our actions. But we are really the ground out of which all thoughts, ideas, and actions spring. In meditation, we come into contact with that ground.

As I sit in meditation, often a thought will arise about what I could have said in class today that would have been better in communicating my message. I can simply observe this thought and let it go. But my natural tendency is to begin a whole chain of thoughts around this one. "Well, can I begin the next class by making this point? Or do I really need to go over that point?" Pretty soon I am in a train of thought such as, "Oh, I didn't do it right. Why can't I think of these things at the right moment? Will I ever be in total command of my teaching?" Once I am on this trip, where has my meditation gone? I have, without being aware, left my comfortable position under the tree and have swum out to the log. Now I'm precariously riding it down the river.

Distractions of this kind can be very tricky. But no matter how long it takes, they must be controlled. And they must not cause us to lose hope. In fact, turn the whole process into a game (just do not turn the game into work). Seeing it as a game will stave off boredom, which is also a major problem.

Expanding Versus Narrowing

Concentration is not the same thing as being in a trance. In a trance, our system is shutting down its reception of information; in concentration—at least in the beginning—we are very much aware of many different stimuli coming into us during meditation. Trance is related to sleep, but concentration could be compared to awakeness or alertness.

Often as people begin to meditate, they're disappointed because nothing special seems to be happening. They know that meditation is an altered state of consciousness, but they believe that they have not succeeded in meditation because they can still hear the traffic noises or because they become aware of other distractions, such as a fly in the room. But they are in an altered state: normally we do not hear traffic noises, and we are not aware of a fly in the room unless it is especially pesky. In meditation, we seek not so much to enter another world as to see this world more fully. This is concentration.

Concentration involves relaxation rather than tension. And this is a tricky state to achieve. Most of us, even if we feel relaxed, are still very tense. In fact, we have to learn how to relax, and then we have to practice frequently. Only when we have really relaxed can we see how tense we usually are.

Concentration is a process that we must let happen. We have to relinquish our need to force it in any way but at the same time we don't surrender the bare concentration to distractions of the moment. Concentration is the work of that balanced totality we are allowing to come to power. We could call this totality the self. The self is a wholeness we don't ordinarily experience, because usually we're controlled and dominated by some smaller component of the self such as the mind or the body. The self is within us and can emerge and assume its rightful control through the practice of concentration. For the self's rightful place is as the integrated center of our being.

Finally, concentration refers to the process of meditation itself. We are not interested in the goal. Concentration happens within the very process of learning to concentrate. It is not a tool that we learn how to handle and then proceed to use. Rather it is a tool we develop in the process of learning to concentrate. It is a tool no one can hand us ready-made; we must fashion it ourselves. And the process itself is sufficient reward for the work of meditation. That is all there is; that is all there need be.

Meditation with a Candle

Over the next week, let's try a new concentration meditation. Do it as often and for as long as you have contracted in your prayer agreement. In a dark room, place a candle about six feet in front of you and look into its flame. We Westerners will be tempted to stare at the candle. This is not meditation. We are searching for a space somewhere between staring (which implies concentrated effort) and daydreaming (which implies relaxation). We are looking for a concentrated relaxation—a relaxed effort. Just allow the candle to be present to you. Let it fill your consciousness, but don't force anything.

Nine

Cultivating Physical Peace

Why the Body?

Our culture has left the body out of our spirituality. The West has no Yoga. There is no great corpus of Western sacred dance. Even in Catholicism, which of all Western religion makes most of the body—through practices such as genuflections, pilgrimages, fasting, and sacraments—there is today very little bodily prayer. While I was studying for the priesthood, the body was looked upon as something to be exercised in sports to keep fit and out of trouble (meaning sexual temptations). Nor are most of us particularly in touch with our bodies. We readers are most likely to be in touch with our minds or our emotions to a greater degree than with our bodies. So it's appropriate to begin our discussion of bodily prayer by asking: can there be any such thing?

Western culture has been living with a split between the body, the spirit, and the mind since the sixth century B.C. About that time, the ideal of the Olympic games—the great symbol of bodily excellence in our culture—began to shift from the idea of physical excellence for everyone to a more restricted idea of a few superb athletes and many spectators. Most people from now on would watch professionals in action rather than engage in the sports themselves. Physical excellence thus began its shift from amateurism (where everyone joined in as best they could) to professionalism (where a gifted few performed for the sedentary many).

As I look at my own feelings concerning my body since I have begun spiritual work, I find that I've never really come to grips with this form that I walk around in and present to the public. Generally I have ignored it, shut it out of awareness, and forgotten I actually have a body. Every so often I come upon a reflection of myself in a store window or a mirror and I say to myself, "Oh, my God, is that what I look like? How awful!" But then the image is gone. Within a few minutes, I have forgotten the whole scene as I continue walking, caught up once again in my mind to where my living really goes on.

I have not been concerned with my body. I'm thankful that it has not provided me with too many problems. On the other hand, I've never been particularly proud of it. I have coexisted with it, considering it neither a great asset nor liability. I have been able to take it for granted. I have never gone to any lengths to take care of it, and I have never attempted to be aware of what it was saying to me.

I never actually expected it to talk to me; if someone had told me that the body talks, I would have looked at them strangely. I'm not a jock; I never played sports when I could avoid them. Physical education in high school was an ordeal. I only learned to swim because once a gym instructor took his job seriously, would not take "I can't" for an answer, and taught me against my will (for which I am grateful).

And then I suddenly realized as I tried to meditate that my body was there. It began interfering with my meditation. And so this dawning awareness of my body led me to the discipline of Yoga. Now Yoga today in this country is almost a fad, Westernized and marketed; you can even watch it on TV. So acclimatized, Yoga is no longer even the in thing to do. It is simply an old and accepted bodily discipline. No American today would go into shock if you told him or her to do Yoga.

But when I first became interested in Yoga, part of the reason was that it was exotic and different. I was attracted because it was a spiritual discipline, not because it was a bodily discipline. (Actually I began Yoga long before I began the spiritual work in earnest.) I wasn't quite sure where the exercises were leading, but I knew they were doing something: they helped me feel relaxed and good. But I had never regarded Yoga as meditation or prayer. In my case, it was simply a very minimal physical exercise somehow linked to Hindu religious practice. I first used Yoga to sleep at night. I was in a pretty noisy environment at graduate school, and only Yoga was able to calm me down enough to sleep.

Now I'm typical of a good number of people. I share with you a real denial of our bodies. We aren't aware of our bodies, and we certainly don't consider our bodies spiritual entities. We're very much a part of the whole philosophy that if there indeed is any spiritual part of us, such as a soul, it has nothing whatsoever to do with our bodies. Many Christians take the very negative attitude that the body is the earthly prison of the soul, which at death will finally be free to fly away. Of course such an attitude is not at all genuinely Christian but, rather, Platonist.

Reclaiming the Body

If we examine the Christian spiritual tradition, the authentic teaching was never one of soul imprisoned in a body, in spite of Puritans' teachings to the contrary. Indeed, in Catholic tradition, the body was quite conspicuously present at worship—signs of the cross, kneeling for prayer, standing for the gospel, fingering rosary beads, and fasting. All such practices as well as the belief in the resurrection of the body (which hopes for a glorified physical body after death), work against the idea that we are a pure soul stuck in a vile container.

We're confronted with a definite task in our spiritual journey: our body must become a part of us—in Christian terms, it must become a worthy temple for the Holy Spirit. I can only fulfill my ambition to pray by allowing my body a vital role in that prayer exercise. If we go back to our definition of prayer as "the opening of ourselves to what is real," then the body plays a crucial role in the opening process. Prayer is a coming alive, it is awakening rather than falling asleep. It means living in the world and being fully alive to it. Fully alive to the world, we at the same time and by the same process become fully alive to ourselves and to God as well.

Are We Ready for Body Prayer?

So how do we go about this bodily prayer, this work on the body? First of all, we must come to the realization that each of us is on a journey, and we are each right now at different stages or points in that journey. Some of you may be much further advanced than I am, some are in about the same place, and some may not have arrived here yet.

We need to know just where we are in our individual journeys. And let's also determine that we will in no way crucify ourselves or short-cut the trip by trying to be where we have not yet arrived. There will be quite enough hardships and even crucifixion along the way without going to look for it. So if you read these words and say you don't know what in the world I'm talking about, if work on the body doesn't yet seem to be a part of praying for you, then accept your attitude as your present stage on the spiritual path. If you see no need to engage in this work right now, there is no need for you to do it. File what you read here for future reference.

In the spiritual journey, we must learn to care for ourselves. We have to become sensitive to exactly where we are in our own pilgrimage. Accepting that point, we begin work from there. Little is gained by taking on some strict regimen that we're not really ready for, don't see the logic of, but hope might be good for us anyway. Such a course of action will get us nowhere.

Believe me, I've gone such a route again and again. In high school, I decided to become physically fit by following the Royal Canadian Air Force exercises. So I went down into the basement and ran my shins into splinters. This program lasted about two weeks, until I decided that life must offer something better than constant pain. I wasn't ready for what exercise had to offer me. And my hard-won advice is that if you're not really ready for something—if the logic and even the necessity and especially the desire are missing from a spiritual project or regimen—reexamine that project and drop it in favor of another that you're genuinely excited about. When you're ready for the next stage of the journey, you'll know; you'll begin to hear about it from yourself.

The Journey as Guide

So as we begin body work, let's agree to do only what we're comfortable with and what we want to do and need to do now. For when we have begun the spiritual journey (and I hope all of us at least do this much now), and if we begin where we're comfortable, then the journey itself, which is a process of opening up to reality, will inform us along the way of each new development. At some point, our body, which perhaps we never heard before, will begin to speak to us about its needs and its condition.

Let me again share a personal example. I began body work with the air force exercises, which were wrong for me, or at least wrong for that time. They were consequently dropped and never attempted again. But then in college, I became interested in Yoga and practiced, not for any lofty purpose, but simply so I could say I was doing something healthy that helped me relax. Besides, I needed no excuse: I enjoyed the Yoga for itself. I was ready for Yoga, which I adopted on my own terms rather than trying to fit myself into some rigid program. So while I have never been tempted to take up the air force exercises again, Yoga has remained a part of my life over the last dozen years.

And Yoga was not originally a form of prayer for me. I never associated the relaxed feelings of well-being that flowed from my practice with prayer at all. I did it for pleasure and because I thought it was good for me. For years, this was the whole extent of my body awareness. Nor was my practice regular and constant. Sometimes Yoga would drop from my life for weeks, months, and even years at a time. But then I would decide to take it up again.

Only a couple of years ago did I finally begin Yoga in earnest, but I still didn't really know what it was all about. (I'm fairly ignorant and dense when it comes to body knowledge.) Within the past year, I've added another body-awareness practice: Kum Nye, or Tibetan relaxation Yoga. In such practices, I have discovered that we must learn to listen to the body. We learn that the body has a whole language of communication that all too often we do not hear.

And as I practiced Yoga and Kum Nye, listening to my body, slowly I began to be aware of my awful posture. It's one thing to know you have poor posture, it's another thing to become aware of it, and it's still another thing to begin work on it. Only within the last few months am I at the point where I want to work on my posture. The technique I use is simple remembering. Whenever I remember my posture, I straighten up, and of course the more I straighten up, the more I remember to straighten up. Naturally five minutes after I have remembered, I have forgotten again, and I return to my usual slouch. But if I can remember often enough, eventually I'll walk straighter.

This task of walking straight (and every other spiritual task) is work, and often hard work at that. Sometimes it might even seem impossible. How many obstacles we have to overcome, and still we can see no end in sight! But there never will be an end in sight. Spiritual work does not run out. It is not a question of doing the work so that we can begin living. Doing the work is really living. Once my posture is straight, I am confident my body will have more work for me to do.

Just lately I have begun to deal with my overweight. Perhaps I can do something about that too. But this is a realization that I had to come to myself, just as with the posture. And in its own good time, when my body knew I was ready and able to hear it, my body suggested I might do something about all this excess baggage. Said my body, "Have you ever considered that you might be a lot better off if I were slimmer?"

I have been so cut off from my body, so out of contact with anything physical, that the things I have just spoken of could only come about because I have reached points in my own spiritual journey where I was able to hear such news and confident enough to do something about it. I encourage you to allow the same process to happen in your life, not only with your body, but in every other aspect of this journey.

Each stage within itself will naturally unfold the succeeding stage. There is an old saying that when a person has progressed to a certain point where she or he needs a teacher, that teacher will appear. But we're not willing to trust the process. We say that if we're to embark upon this trip, we first have to find an enlightened master who can guide us each step of the way. So we spend all our time looking for this teacher and never actually find him or her. The truth is that the enlightened master is within each of us and—like a good teacher—will not overwhelm us but will reveal one small step at a time. And when we have awakened to hear and carry out that one step, then we'll be ready to hear and undertake the next. If at any time we need help from the outside, let's trust that we'll find that help: when we really need the teacher, the teacher will appear. And we'll also be ready to receive what the teacher has to give us. For, if we're not prepared for the teacher, then even if we listen we won't hear, because we're not able to assimilate what we listen to.

Centering

Centeredness is one of the major concepts of body work, so it would aid us to investigate this idea. Following the traditional spiritualities, let's narrow down the possible centers to three.

• The first is in the head and the brain. People centered here work primarily through the intellect and reasoning powers. The caricature is the egghead. When this person refers to *I*, he or she is really speaking of his or her intellect. My own self-image used to be of a brain that was carried around and serviced by the rest of my body. But the brain and to a certain extent my head (eyes, ears, nose, and mouth) were the only really alive parts of me.

• If, on the other hand, you're very in touch with your emotions, you'll picture your center around the heart, which traditionally has been considered the seat of the emotions.

Although we're using metaphorical language when we speak of centers, the image is not just metaphorical. The center is truly a center, even in the matter of gravity. Brain people have a center of gravity very high off the ground. Thus it is fairly easy to knock them over. And they seem to delight in being overturned, as witness their love of debate and argument.

But the heart person has a much lower center of gravity, so he or she is not so easily toppled as the intellectual. Indeed, the heart person can sway back and forth much more without losing his or her sense of balance. And we could say that the person working from the emotions is much more malleable and able to bend than the person working out of intellect alone.

• Finally, if you are a person who centers in the physical body, you'll discover your center point just below the navel. The traditional organ in Western tradition for the body feelings is the liver, and Europeans even today show much more care and concern with the proper health and functioning of their livers than do we Americans. If your center is in this lower region when you are aware of and living in touch with your body, then you have a low enough center of gravity to prevent you from being thrown over. You can roll with the forces that crash into you.

Finding the Three Centers

Perhaps all this talk of centering sounds too physical. But it is indeed physical. And if you'll only take the time to open yourself to these ideas experimentally, you'll be able to verify in your own life these spiritual teachings. Let's sit down now and take five to ten minutes to find out where our being is centered right now. Each of us is generally centered in one of these places. But at times, we experience a shift in our center of gravity. When we're reading, we're usually centered in the head. When we play football or other sports, we probably are centered in the navel. When we're in love, we're centered in the heart. Where are you centered right now? Where do you actually feel your center of gravity, your real being, right now? During the week, as you engage in other activities, take a moment in the midst of that activity to notice what center you're operating out of. With just a little practice, you can become aware of these centers, and you can eventually shift the center as you wish.

The Body Never Lies

Spiritual teaching says the body never lies. Indeed, this is the basis for such a scientific device as the lie detector. We all know that words can lie constantly. Sometimes we don't even know whether we're speaking truth or falsehood. But the body knows, and the lie detector picks up the body's response.

When we enter on the spiritual journey or even just the ordinary

62

living of life, we often come upon the question of what is true. In meditation, we wonder about the validity of certain experiences. They occur in such a subtle area that we can't be sure whether they are real experiences or whether we're only deceiving ourselves. But if we can enter our body center so that we can experience from that center, we'll be able to tell truth from delusion.

Most of us, I believe, are not body people. If you're like me, the experience of being really centered in the body is new and strange. This experience is felt whenever we're totally involved in some activity or sport so that we're running on automatic pilot. We're not asleep; in fact, we feel very much alive. But we have a sense that the body is performing on its own, very efficiently and very accurately. Unfortunately, it is an experience that usually can't be taught by book. But there are enough teachers and techniques around for you not to feel abandoned or on your own.

Being in the body is for me a new way of existing—a different way of being in the world. I'm so accustomed to being in my head all the time that when I slip into the emotions or body feelings, I think that I've actually fallen. But in truth, the mind is the worst place to discover truth. The body is best because it doesn't have the cunning to deceive. The emotions (which lie between the body and the mind) partake in some truthfulness and some deceit.

Centering Exercise

Many different exercises can produce centeredness. Take some time alone in a quiet place to experiment with walking. First walk in your normal fashion. Then, as you walk, imagine the center of your being a few inches below the navel. Place your attention and your consciousness there. Pretty soon you will begin to feel the difference.

In all these exercises, it is important for you to believe in what we're talking about. If you're not open to believing in centeredness, it will be harder, if not impossible, for you to be open to the experience. So for the sake of the experiment, believe and take an attitude of play and experimentation. You'll learn nothing as long as you simply continue reading this book.

It doesn't matter that you lack a clear idea of centeredness. Experiment with it anyway. Eventually your experience will clarify the matter. What your mind entertains as possible, you'll find can happen to you. If your mind is not open to something, you'll find it difficult if not impossible to experience that thing.

63

If there are no miracles today, perhaps it's because we have no room for them. We refuse to consider them as a possibility, and so we don't recognize the potential for miracles and allow them to occur.

May the Force Be with You

Another concept quite strange to modern thinking is the energy body. This idea is presented in *The Teachings of Don Juan*. The writer, Carlos Castenada, begins as a UCLA anthropology student interested in the ritual uses of peyote among the Indians of the Southwest. He tries to get Don Juan, a Yaqui Indian sorcerer, to reveal to him his knowledge of peyote. Instead, Don Juan makes Carlos a disciple and teaches him to be a man of knowledge.

But before accepting Carlos, Don Juan puts him through a test to discover whether he's worthy and teachable. Don Juan leads Carlos onto the front porch, where he will spend the night. He must find a space on that porch that is beneficial and right for him. By implication, there is also a space that is unfavorable to him. Carlos reacts like a typical Westerner; he is annoyed and angry that Don Juan should subject him to such a ridiculous task. After all, in our world, any space can be either good or bad; actually all space is neutral. But Carlos desperately wants the peyote information only Don Juan can give him. So he undertakes his vigil.

As the night proceeds, Carlos imagines he can detect differences in various parts of the porch. Although he's sure his mind is just playing games, he has no choice but to go along if he wishes any chance of interviewing Don Juan. Toward morning, he believes he may have discovered his place, so he sits there. Don Juan emerges from the house to congratulate a weary and doubtful Carlos on having found his spot and passed the test.

Don Juan's world is not limited by the same bounds as our own. We assume that what cannot be seen, heard, or measured doesn't exist. And when someone tells us of worlds not perceivable by the ordinary eye, we immediately dismiss him as primitive and hung up in magic. But is he? Throughout history Don Juan has much better company than we do: all major religious figures including Jesus would align themselves with Don Juan. Every true spirituality teaches that there is more in heaven and earth than can be dreamt of in ordinary human philosophy and science.

Underlying this teaching of Don Juan is the concept that there are subtle energies at work in the world that ordinary waking consciousness is too gross to perceive but that can be received by a properly trained consciousness. In Christianity, we meet similar concepts in the idea of angels (beings who are pure spirit) and in the soul (another name for energy body, perhaps?). There are other entities besides the physical body, and our life does not end with the physical body's death. Such spiritual teaching reaches back at least to Plato in Europe and far earlier in the East.

We can experiment with this idea in a simple way. For example, we commonly believe that our body is bound by the layer of skin that keeps the organs and tissues in place. The skin is the physical boundary, but it is not the absolute boundary of our being.

The Energy Body

Take some time to calm yourself. Then, in this relaxed state of mind and with your eyes closed, slowly bring your hands together. Can you feel when the energy body is reached? With a little practice and belief, you'll soon be able to feel the energy that emanates from your body a few inches out from your skin.

When you have discovered this new body, begin to explore and come to know it. Give yourself an energy massage. Sit upright with crossed legs in a relaxed state of consciousness. Then slowly massage your legs with your palms. Do not touch the legs. Rather massage the energy body about three inches out from the skin. As you grow more able to perceive this body, you can begin to read it.

Find out which parts of the energy body are hot and cold. Find out how to recognize tension through feeling the energy body. Give a massage to other parts of your body, or find a partner and give one another energy back massages. Then share with one another what you felt during the massage.

Belief in this concept of energy body can teach us many things about our body and its health, illnesses, and tensions. Simply expand what you'll allow to exist within your world. If you allow for the possibility of a subtle body in addition to the physical one, and if you'll come to know and communicate with that body, its reality will become readily apparent.

The energy body is already coming to be more widely known and accepted. The popular film *Star Wars* brings the idea into mass entertainment, and the Force (as it is called there) is responsible for much of the story's appeal. The Force is the good energy of the universe to which the knights of old belonged and which they served. In the film, the young man Luke is taught how to trust in the Force rather than in his own senses. In the film's climax, Luke must perform the almost impossible task of firing a missile from a speeding rocket into a small passageway on the death star. He succeeds, not by following the information supplied by his senses or even by the computers, but by surrendering himself to the Force so that the Force may work through him.

All these ideas—the Force, the special place on the porch, the energy body—are specific instances of a teaching that views the world as more than can be seen by the naked untaught senses. Whatever the body work we engage in, we'll come upon some such teaching. It behooves us at least to know that such a concept exists and also to be open to such an idea: it is not inherently ridiculous.

No good teacher will demand that we accept such notions totally on faith. All they ask is that we be open to such notions and willing to entertain and test them. Like Luke Skywalker in *Star Wars*, we will discover that although they seem far out and bizarre compared to our "common-sense" view of the world, nevertheless they point to a reality. There is a body within and beyond us that can be more in touch with the world than we are through our senses and intelligence alone.

A Matter of Fine Tuning

Many of us enter the spiritual journey seeking special exotic experiences. Such horizons first appeared to Americans through the drug culture. There were accounts of seeing God, of leaving the body behind, of traveling through the bloodstream, and of many other weird and wonderful adventures. Drugs merely opened the door and showed us that such experiences were possible. But then we found that these experiences were available through means other than drugs. And so many people embarked upon the spiritual journey in search of these broader worlds of vision.

The secret of such experiences lies in making our perceptions more and more refined and subtle. The laughter of angels can be heard right here and now. But we need to open ourselves in order to hear it. Our senses now are very gross; unless a perception comes up and smacks us in the face, so to speak, we don't notice it. We're not attuned to all the very fine stimuli in our environment, so we miss much of what is happening all around us.

But the Judeo-Christian tradition teaches that God more often than not reveals himself through subtle events rather than through grand

and overwhelming miracles. Elijah the prophet seeks to hear the voice of God. So he waits, and the whirlwind comes. But God is not in the wind. The fire comes, but God is not there. Finally Elijah hears God in a still small voice. If his hearing had not been finely tuned, he would have missed the voice of God altogether. How many of us have hearing that could find God in the still small voice of our own life? If we, like Elijah, could become one with our bodies, we might hear that voice instead of lamenting that God doesn't speak today.

Many traditional disciplines provide ways into body work. Yoga is available today at almost every YMCA. However, it's important to find a teacher who practices Yoga as a spiritual discipline, not just as a special exercise in physical fitness. Most Yoga taught in this country is a bastardized form that merely considers itself a series of easy stretching postures that lead to relaxation and well-being. Such a simplification is not harmful, but it does miss much of what Yoga offers in its approach to meditation and spirituality.

The Japanese and Chinese martial arts such as Aikido and Tai Chi are also body spiritualities. Tai Chi is known as the gentlest of the martial arts and resembles a cross between self-defense and flowing dance. Arica, a modern school of spirituality, teaches a form of body work known as Psychocalisthenics: a blend of Yoga, calisthenics, and other body disciplines aimed at awakening the psychic faculties. There is also a Tibetan form of Yoga known as Kum Nye, which focuses awareness on the subtle body.

Books are available on all these disciplines, but it is best to learn through actual contact with a teacher. Books should only be a last resort, and, if used, must be followed with extreme attention and care. It is so easy to miss the point when reading, because these are very subtle teachings.

Such knowledge has traditionally been secret not simply because people do not wish to share it, but because not all people are at a stage of human development where they could appreciate and understand it. These teachings are secret because such knowledge cannot be indiscriminately publicized in books but can only be communicated from one human being to another through sharing and communion. In such disciplines, we learn to perceive very small stimuli and very delicate changes. Learning plain and obvious things is relatively easy, but it is difficult to refine the senses and perceive what is normally invisible and unacknowledged.

Here is an example from my Kum Nye practice, many of whose exercises are extremely simple and involve no effort to do. We might say that nothing is happening in them. The discipline of Kum Nye, however, teaches us to look at these very simple movements and observe what is actually happening. The essence of Kum Nye is not to do the exercises in some narrowly prescribed way but rather to be aware of whatever is happening in the body during the movement. Normally we would not pay attention to such "insignificant" stimuli.

In one class, we stood up with our arms stretched above our heads. There we stood, and we stood. And we stood. After about ten minutes, I became angry. I realized the last time I had been like this was in primary school when I had misbehaved. What was I doing in this painful position thirty years later, feeling like an idiot and paying money for such an experience besides?

We then proceeded to the second movement of the exercise: slowly we lowered our arms, crossed the palms, and placed them over our hearts. Now I experienced wonderful feelings of love and compassion flowing from my heart. I was suspicious of them, of course. I kept telling myself that really I only felt relieved of the pain: like the person in the proverb, I bang my head against the wall because it feels so good when I stop.

After we'd spent a few minutes in this posture, the instructor asked us to sit down and share with one another what we had experienced during this exercise. When it was my turn, I shared the feelings of love and compassion I'd felt. Then the instructor asked if that was all I had felt. So I shared some of my skepticism. I should accept skepticism, she said, as a genuine feeling and as a part of my experience. Then she asked if there was anything else. "Well," I said, "actually there is, but it's not important."

"Why don't you share it anyway?" she suggested.
"Well, if you really want to know, I felt damn mad and ripped off."
"That is great," she said. "That is as genuine a part of your experience as the feelings of love."

Suddenly I realized how I deny my feelings by judging them as inadequate, unworthy, or simply wrong. If we're to listen to our bodies and hear their soft voices, we must stop this constant process of criticism and censorship. Every experience is valid and true just because it is experience. We must listen to our experiences and learn from them rather than prevent them from even coming into consciousness.

Distractions are a great frustration in prayer. But they are also a normal part of prayer and should be accepted as such. Something is happening, something is being communicated in that distraction. Why not get into it? Did you ever consider meditating on the distraction to find out what it is really like? Nothing need be distraction. Everything can be meditation, including the distractions. Treat your distractions as objects of meditation just as you used a candle. It is a dead end to believe meditation occurs only when we sit down in our corner on our meditation cushion, shut our eyes, and concentrate upon the breath. But Yoga, Tai Chi, Kum Nye, jogging, golf, tennis, swimming, and walking are also meditation if only we practice being awake during them.

Fasting and Almsgiving

Christianity is not rich in body prayer, but it does offer the discipline of fasting. If, like most Americans, you have a weight problem, fasting might be worth a try. Fasting, of course, means different things: (1) total abstinence from all food, or (2) restriction of the diet to just one food (usually a fruit juice), or (3) the old Catholic idea of one main meal and two smaller meals a day. All are called fasts. In this book, I'm talking about fasts of the first or second variety. And for this reason, the fasts would last only a day or at most three days.

But why should fasting be spiritual? First, it cleanses the body and gives a rest to the digestive system. Foods, in addition to being nutritious, are also poisonous or produce toxins in our system.

Second, fasting takes us out of our ordinary routine. And from this new vantage point, we can reexamine our lives and especially our eating habits. We very easily eat ourselves into a rut—eating merely for the sake of eating. Sometimes we don't even know whether we're truly hungry or are just eating for the social or habitual reasons. But fasting breaks us from this routine and allows us to evaluate and modify our habits. It also renews our appreciation of food. Abstinence makes the palate grow fonder.

The idea of three square meals a day as a minimum for survival is nonsense. And fasting rightly carried out is not starvation. In my own rather limited experience of fasting, I have found that there is no real hunger. And rather than feeling tired and weak, I find myself with reserves of energy I don't normally feel.

Fasting clears us and gives us what popular language calls a high. Meditation during a fast is often a much richer experience than normal. For one thing, the body is more at rest: it's not working to transform food into energy. We feel lighter and clearer; there is less distraction.

69

Of course fasting is not something you should rush into. First of all, be sure that you really want to fast and that you'll be comfortable with the fast. Second, how you begin and leave the fast are important considerations. To end a three-day fast with a big steak dinner is to be cruel to your body. Finally, be sure that for any fast longer than three days, you're under a doctor's supervision. But right now, I'm talking about just a one-day fast, or at most a two-day fast, every so often as a means of breaking the routine of our lives and turning inside.

We might also consider the advantages of fasting over dieting. Unless your spirituality despises the world, one goal of your spiritual journey should be to enjoy the world. But how can the person on a constant diet enjoy the world? Many of the foods he or she most wants to eat are forbidden. Such a person must say that sugar is bad, or butter and lobster are too rich. How can this person enjoy and celebrate the goodness of the creation if the most tempting foods are off-limits?

But the person who fasts does so in order to purify herself or himself and keep body weight in check. Fasting modifies and regulates the appetite so that when the person returns to ordinary eating patterns there is no tendency to eat more than needed. A look at our waistlines will show us how much we do tend ordinarily to eat more than necessary.

But neither does he have to deny himself the things he likes. He enjoys them in moderation, and he celebrates the goodness of the earth in his feasting. The Christian who fasts moderately throughout Lent can experience and fully celebrate the great feast of Easter with a cleansed palate and renewed appreciation for the food of God's earth.

Developing Body Awareness

Here is a simple body-awareness exercise to practice. It doesn't build the body or slim it down or massage it or stretch the muscles: it is solely an exercise in learning to listen to the body. Take off any belt or clothing that restricts movement, especially around the abdomen.

Stand up straight and close your eyes for a few moments. Focus your awareness upon your breath, and relax. Then begin to bend forward, starting with the head. Pretend you are bending each vertebra separately as you slowly bend forward all the way over so that your hands touch the floor in front of your feet. Bend only as far forward as possible without bending your knees. Hold this position for a minute or so. All during this exercise—which is done as slowly as possible—you want your attention focused upon what is happening in your body. Feel every movement as fully as possible. Be aware of any energy in the body. Notice your thoughts and feelings during the entire exercise. Are there any memories or feelings that arise during the exercise?

After a moment or so, very slowly begin to straighten up again, unbending each vertebra one by one from the bottom of the spine up through the top of the neck. When you're upright, continue the movement by bending backward. Bend back only as far as is comfortable. Then hold that backward position for a moment, remembering to scan your body, thoughts, and feelings. Now slowly come back to the upright position. Rest and relax in your standing position for a moment or two, again scanning the body, mind, and feelings.

After doing this exercise briefly, jot down in your prayer diary what you experienced. Be brief, but don't censor or judge. Then go through the entire process two more times, and record any experiences each time in the diary. Over the next week or so, do this threefold bend each day and record the experiences. You may be surprised at the wealth of experiences called forth by this simple process. This practice of being attentive, although it might seem too easy or superficial, is the necessary work that must be done so that our attention may be sharpened. And the discipline of recording our experiences in the journal helps us keep alive and prevents the routine from falling into a mere physical exercise done halfheartedly and, more important, half-attentively.

Ten

Cultivating Spiritual Peace

Cultivation of the spirit is the hardest of our three exercises. Though prayer is primarily a spiritual activity, the disciplining of the mind and body in prayer is a much easier task than the disciplining of the spirit. The spirit is subtle. Unlike the body, it can't be touched or felt. It doesn't make its presence known like the mind by filling us with constant chatter. Spirit is not the body nor the mind. But many people today believe that if you remove the body and the mind, nothing is left. Spirit is hard for us to deal with because our civilization doesn't believe in it.

What are we looking for when we seek spirit? Breath is a powerful symbol for spirit in a number of religions traditions. Hinduism links spirit to breath, less substantial than the body but more than the mind. Jesus in John's Gospel calls spirit breath and wind. He remarks on its mystery—it goes and moves where it will. Hebrew uses the same word for breath and spirit: *ruach*. Greek does the same: *pneuma*. And if the spirit blows where it wills, how independent and elusive it is—so elusive that over the past few hundred years, we in the West have denied it any existence.

To enter into the spiritual work, we must at least entertain the notion of spirit, even if we have no experience of it and aren't ready to accept its reality on faith. At least we have the assurance of every major religious and spiritual tradition that there is a spiritual reality, even though our science has not included spirit in its notion of the world.

Let's entertain the possibility that spirit exists and then seek to find in our experience evidence and proof of its existence. Let's use our life as our laboratory. We will learn to tune into and be aware of what is spiritual in our lives. For the spirit is present, but it is so quiet and hidden that unless we know where and how to look for it, we're apt to miss it entirely and accept the false belief that it really doesn't exist.

Our experiment must proceed in a rather roundabout way. Praying people are whole and integrated. So in order to cultivate the spirit, we don't need to work upon the spirit directly, but rather we can pursue the work we have already begun on the mind and body. As we progress with this work on the more obvious dimensions of our being, the presence of the spiritual will begin to show itself.

In this book, a product of human thought, the work of prayer is broken up to fit a conceptual scheme of mind, body, and spirit. But there are no such neat divisions and compartments in the life and practice of prayer. The first requirement of our praying is to become attentive to who we are, where we are, and what our own private journey is. As we make that journey, we can begin to discern elements that relate to neither mind nor body but come under the aegis of spirit. But remind yourself again about the rules against rushing the journey, against judging your own work, and against despairing of progress, which we outlined in the chapter on body work. If we pay close attention to our journey, knowing what to look for, we will soon see signs of the spirit.

Relaxation

The first path to spiritual awareness is though relaxation. Tension is a primary obstacle to our awareness of spirit. Most of us probably would deny we're tense. But it's not a matter of having the jitters or being on prescriptions for tranquilizers. Just living within American society makes survival almost impossible without a great deal of tension. Tension is a constant factor in our lives; we're no longer even aware of its presence. We tune it out to attend to other stimuli in about the same way we tune out our awareness of our breathing.

If we live with constant tension, we can't possibly know we're tense; we don't know life without tension. Relaxation is foreign to us. Something constant is accepted as normal. A constant headache would pretty soon simply be accepted as part of being human. We'd tune it out, compensate for it, and try to live a decent life in spite of it. We must learn to cope with tension so constant and pervasive that even our attempts at relaxation are filled with it. The average American vacation is almost as hurried and harried as the rest of our lives. Only the routine changes, but the driving energy to do something, to see as much as possible, to enjoy ourselves to the fullest, cramming every moment with new experiences, is hardly conducive to relaxation.

Most of our tension is unseen. We cannot really begin to recognize it until we experience relaxation. And we're so imbued with tension that relaxation no longer comes naturally. We have to learn it. If we were told to go and relax right now, most of us would probably go to a couch or a bed and lie down. And we would think that this lying down is all there is to relaxation. Yet chances are that lying down will relax us only a little more than our degree of tension right now. The tension does not diminish.

But there are easy techniques that can teach us how to relax. And once we've caught a glimpse of real relaxation, we can build upon that experience, going deeper and deeper into relaxation. We can then also acknowledge the tension that forms a part of our life, and we can learn to control and use that tension. I don't advocate getting rid of the tension. That would make functioning in our society impossible. But we can learn to use the tension when we need it, then turn it off when it's not useful.

When I am in the midst of a situation, I'm very much unaware of what my body is saying or of what my emotions are saying. If you stopped me in the heat of argument and asked if I were tense, I'd have to think about it, even if only for a split second. For I am unaware of the tension that is spilling out in the heat of the moment. If I'm really out of touch with myself, I may not even acknowledge my tension. I may vehemently deny it altogether, becoming angry and even more tense for having my tension spotlighted.

But as we practice relaxation, we can build a gauge or thermometer that will tell when we're indeed tense. Acknowledged tension can be controlled and used. Tension, although we need it in order to cope with modern life, does very little good in itself. It keeps us ignorant of ourselves, of what we're feeling, of who we truly are. Imagine we're made out of rubber, like little rubber toys children play with. Tension stretches us apart, elongating and distorting our bodies. If we live with this tension long enough, we begin to assume that this weird stretched shape is actually our true form. But take the rubber doll out of the stretching machine and it bounces back to its normal dimensions and appearance. The doll is elongated and strained only because the tension is holding it there. It's the same with us. We might think of tension as noise. When we spoke of silence, we saw how noise fills our lives and keeps the silence out. Well, tension is probably the most prevalent noise in our lives.

A Relaxation Technique

Relaxation techniques are easily available in our culture. Here is a simple one from the Yoga system. Lie on a couch or bed, or even the floor. Close your eyes. Then progressively tense the different parts of your body. Begin with the feet and legs. Lift each leg in turn about six inches from the floor, hold it straight out, and tense it. When you apply the tension, take a deep breath and hold it. After a few seconds, release the tension and the breath, letting the leg fall back to the floor lifeless. Continue the process, moving up the body to the buttocks, stomach, and chest (take in a breath and hold it first down in the abdomen; breathe out; then take another breath into the chest cavity), hands and arms, shoulders, neck, and finally the face (first stretch all the face in toward the nose, puckering up as much as possible, then pull all the skin away from the center, feeling the skin really stretch, open your eyes as far as possible, open the mouth as wide as possible, and stick out your tongue; then repeat the process of pulling the face in toward the center again).

If you set aside twenty minutes to do this exercise and deepen your relaxation, you'll find it more beneficial than a short nap. Once you've successively tensed and relaxed each part of the body, return over the different parts of the body again, this time using your mind to scan each part for tension. As you scan, suggest that each part can relax even more.

We're practicing a form of self-hypnosis, giving suggestions to our body. Success depends on our confidence that it will work. Be open, and allow the relaxation to happen. And when you're relaxed, enjoy it for a while. Explore it and come to know what it's like. But don't drift off to sleep. Maintain consciousness throughout the relaxation by placing your attention on the breath. This approach will keep you awake and at the same time allow the relaxation to deepen even further.

When you come out of this deep relaxation, first tell yourself to remember how you got there, and assure yourself that you can return to this state any time you wish. When you've given yourself this suggestion, then slowly bring yourself back to ordinary consciousness. But take your time, and imagine the energy returning to your body through your breath. The breath will stimulate you as it sends this tingling energy into your body, down through the legs and arms. Only when you feel fully refreshed should you open your eyes and then slowly sit up.

Each time you practice this relaxation, you'll find it becoming easier for you and you'll learn how to relax even more. When you're in this special realm of deep relaxation, you can begin to experience yourself as you really are without the troubles and tensions of daily life that always buzz about as you go about your daily rounds.

Working on Consciousness

Examination of conscience is the traditional Christian term for what we will call examination of consciousness. The traditional practice often became more moralistic than spiritual: it was a time to consider how many sins were committed that day, or—less often—how many virtues were practiced. Such an examination is too narrow. Ignatius of Loyola, who developed this technique, was concerned with an inventory of the whole of consciousness.

Take about ten minutes at the end of your day, when you can be alone. Consider everything that happened that day. You might tell the day as a story to yourself. Relive as much of the day as possible. Consider events, conversations, thoughts, feelings, and especially the quality of consciousness during any specific period.

How conscious was I during that conversation? How awake was I to what was happening? To get a handle on the day, you might ask, "How has this day been unique in my life? How did I feel, and how did I respond and react today? What was my body like—my mind, my spirit? How much of today was spent in sleep and not really conscious (not necessarily in bed or with the eyes closed)?"

Avoid asking "why" questions. This is not the time for fault finding or for congratulations. Your goal is merely to bring the day into consciousness so that you can see it for what it was and enjoy it now in tranquility.

By reviewing the day and bringing it into consciousness, we can actually begin to live fuller lives. There is no need to punish ourselves or reward ourselves either. The mere fact that we review the day is quite enough to start a change in daily life. We become more aware of the times we're sleeping, of how we respond to people and situations, of the opportunities for living and growing that each day provides. If we enter this review in our journal, we can observe the concrete progress from week to week.

76

Another technique is considerably more difficult than the examination, but its rewards are considerably richer. This is the practice of consciousness itself. Spiritual teachers say we go through life asleep. In the Christian Gospels, the disciples are asleep during the most crucial moments of Jesus' life. They sleep through the storm at sea, the transfiguration, and the garden of agony. A Sufi aphorism goes: "O you who fear the difficulties of the road to annihilation—do not fear. It is so easy, this road, that it may be travelled sleeping."

In this exercise, you practice being fully awake to the world for ten minutes a day. The time need not be an important one, and there is no need to stop your normal routine for this practice. You can do it while washing dishes, or teaching a class, or driving a car. The important element is the conscious decision to practice being fully awake for these ten minutes.

During that time, be as fully present as is possible to whatever is happening. If you're doing some task, you'll be fully awake to that task rather than falling into daydreams or thinking of something else. You want to avoid lapsing into either the past or the future during this exercise: you want to be totally involved in the present moment. During this time, you'll be as fully aware as possible of what you're seeing, hearing, feeling, and so on. You open all your senses and sensitivities to whatever you're presently engaged upon.

Normally we forget that it is *I* who am involved in this life. The forgetting of this *I* makes us egocentric. We assume that whatever is happening is happening to the universe and not just to us. But when we become conscious of our *I*, we begin to see the world truly from our individual perspective. We're alive to our own unique vision and experience. When we're aware of our presence in a situation, we're more alive to that situation, and there is more of us there to be involved. A large part of us (including the *I*) is not off sleeping somewhere while we maneuver on automatic pilot.

When I am not aware of my *I*, things are just happening. I'm walking down Telegraph Avenue on my way to a store. At that moment, I am really not aware of myself. All I'm conscious of are the sights, sounds, and feelings coming upon me. I have forgotten myself as a real-life human being within this situation. Instead, I am an empty shell walking along receiving different stimuli. But *I* am not fully there.

If during your exercise of being fully present you continually remind yourself that you're seeing, and you're feeling, and you're walking, and you're tasting, then you acquire an alarm clock to wake you up. And this ten-minute exercise acts as a leaven in the rest of the day. Real spirituality is not something we practice alone for only a certain period each day. Real spirituality refers to our life each minute. We withdraw in order to practice being alive. But we practice, not for the practice itself, but so that in each situation of our real life we might be more awake, alive, and spiritual.

Ego Training

We might also practice letting go of the ego. I define ego as whatever in me is grasping and selfish. The ego would like me to believe I'm the center of the universe. It separates *me* from *you*. Let's take grasping as our central concept. Quite a complete definition of ego is this: whatever in me wants to hold on to or possess people, things, feelings, memories, relationships. The opposite is an attitude of letting go and giving freedom to the world.

The ego must not be destroyed. Actually it would be impossible for any of us to survive in the world without it. But its domination and hold over our life must be weakened. Christianity and other religions provide a number of such ego-weakening techniques.

In the last chapter, we looked at fasting as spiritual work. Fasting teaches the body its place in the human person and also purifies and strengthens it so that it might assume its proper role. In Christianity, two disciplines closely associated with fasting—denial and alms giving—work on the ego in much the same way fasting disciplines the body.

Jesus is not ambivalent about the ego: "Whoever does not deny himself, take up his cross, and follow me cannot enter into the kingdom of God." And to deny oneself is to deny that part that grasps.

We don't like denying ourselves. It's not fashionable today. And there are very good reasons for being cautious and skeptical toward denial. It often turns into masochism. Wearing the hair shirt and whipping the body were morbid expressions of hatred for the body and the flesh. Masochism is involved whenever the feeling behind denial is something like, "O wretched me, I'm such a creep, I really should heap dirt on myself because I deserve no better."

But the spiritual discipline of denial is not masochism. Denial is a way of working on ourselves. We have this ego, this grasping mechanism that wants to possess the entire world and place itself as God in the center. But the ego is not God, nor is it even the godlike part of our makeup. It is not the urge to be like God that is wrong. What's wrong is that we seek to become God under the banner of the ego, which is incapable of carrying out the task. Ego is the major obstacle toward our God-consciousness; it must be denied if we're to make any progress.

We deny the ego by first taking a critical look at ourselves. We must come to see just where we're vulnerable. We must also understand exactly what we are capable of.

If you're a four-pack-a-day smoker and your life depends on those smokes, that's not the right place to begin denial, even though it is an outstanding enslavement. Look first for what you can afford to give up right now. What are you ready and willing to part with? Each of us must be alert and sensitive to our own path. And we proceed slowly and gradually. Thus we gradually build up our strength little by little for the harder encounters ahead.

Two years ago when I entered upon this journey, I never thought of dieting. If I had even been aware that I was overweight and decided to act, I would probably have failed. I wasn't yet strong enough to deny myself sweets. But today I feel ready. In my own time, I have realized I'm too big and have decided I don't wish to remain this way. So I'm now ready and able to shed those pounds.

Surprisingly enough, I've done it without much difficulty or regret. The pleasure and pride far "outweigh" the pain and frustrations. But it still involves denial. It means saying to my ego that it doesn't need all that ice cream. It means exerting a force over my wants and even my needs—a force that sees a higher good than simple immediate gratification. This work, secular as it seems, is deeply spiritual if we'll only be aware of the spiritual aspects of the work.

What can you let go of right now? Even if something is very obvious, don't confront it until you have the insight, the strength, and the energy to win the fight. With one step at a time, we can complete section after section of the journey. But if we take a great leap, we may wind up breaking our legs and being bogged down indefinitely. Have no fear. There's no unemployment in this work; there's plenty to keep each of us busy from now until the hour of our deaths.

Almsgiving is a traditional work on the ego. Part of our grasping attitude involves money. Almsgiving reminds us that money is not the ultimate in our life, and it helps us cultivate a certain detachment from our money. We give to those less fortunate than ourselves. And the beauty of almsgiving is not only the charity but also the detachment we discover that enables us to use ourselves and our goods in less ego-gratifying ways than we might normally do.

Discerning the Spirit

Discernment of spirits is a notion that descends from Ignatius of Loyola, but I'll use it in a rather larger context than is traditional in Christianity. This is a subtle and advanced exercise. As I mentioned before, we find it difficult to discern whether we even have a spirit, let alone any differences in spirits. Angels and demons, good and bad spirits—these are common to all religions. Such ideas are valid insights into the nature of the world, in spite of the mythological trappings in which they are clothed—trappings that provide angels with wings and demons with cloven hooves, tails, and pitchforks.

Within the universe are good and evil forces that are not limited to human beings. These forces usually manifest their power in people, but they also go beyond the purely personal incarnations. I'm not implying that there's a devil or a force of evil that's equal to the force of good. Nor does this view give credence to all the hysterical furor over demon possession and exorcism. Christian teaching about spirits is that no evil spirit has any real power compared to the power of God—that the only real power they possess is that given them by people. Perhaps it is easier for us to grasp what is meant by spirits through our concept of moods. Often I feel I'm not in control of my moods. I wake up depressed, and I can't find out why I should be depressed. This mood seems to come upon me from outside. More primitive people attributed these moods to the influence of spirits. We may not accept their explanation, but we do know the reality they were pointing out.

As our work on mind, body, and spirit progresses, we come upon stages when we need to evaluate ourselves and come to some understanding of where we are and where we're headed. Are we making progress? Are we going down the wrong path? Are we deceiving ourselves?

We'll have times of exhilaration, which Ignatius calls times of consolation. At other times, we'll experience desolation. Work in dieting provides such experiences. The first couple of weeks, we're consoled as we see the pounds drop away. But then when nothing happens the third and fourth week and the scale stays at the same weight, we experience the unhappiness of desolation: "I'm stuck. Nothing's happening. It's all for nothing."

How are we to work with consolation and desolation on this journey? Ignatius advises us never to make a decision when we're in desolation. Only in the state of consolation can we make balanced decisions, because then we're not ruled by negative feelings and thoughts. When we're depressed (and that is another name for desolation), we're in no position to make a good decision: the world is distorted through the depression. Everything looks bleak and cheerless. Nothing has any great purpose or meaning.

But discernment goes beyond consolation and desolation. It can help us evaluate whether our experiences upon the path help or harm our further development. For the sake of simplicity, let's consider three rules for the discernment and evaluation of any spiritual experience. Such evaluation must not be undertaken lightly or frequently. But there is a need periodically to take a look at our work on ourselves. Otherwise we fall into routines and ruts, wandering far from the path because—in a sense—we have fallen asleep at the wheel.

• The first rule of discernment concerns integration of mind, body, and spirit. If while working on our task of self-transformation we narrow our perspective to just the mind or body or spirit, and nothing is happening in the other areas, then we're in trouble. This is not to say we never concentrate on one of these areas. Our spirituality at times will be heavily centered in the body. But that shouldn't mean that development ceases in the mind and the spirit. Such experiences are a normal proper way of working. I'm talking about a narrowing of the work that sometimes occurs when somebody decides that the body or the spirit or the mind is unimportant or has no share in achieving the final goal toward which we travel.

Such a failure of integration often occurs within drug spiritualities. When psychedelic drugs are used as the only way of exploring the spirit, the mind expands. But the spirit is often unable to grasp and understand the various experiences. Thus the pilgrimage becomes merely a trip—freaky experiences that gain nothing. The experiences, valid and real in their own right, can't be integrated into the person's life to transform and enrich it. It's like showing diagrams of some advanced mathematics or physics to a child of three. The child may be fascinated by all the beautiful lines and may even attempt to play with them, but she or he is totally incapable of assimilating and dealing with their meaning. So LSD and other psychedelic drugs can take us into spiritual realms that we simply don't have the wisdom to be able to appropriate into our own life. The spiritual experience, cut off from our everyday world, becomes a mere fantasy trip or escape from reality.

The drug trip also goes against the principle of integration in terms of the body. The ingestion of these chemicals shocks the physical system. The body is taken into experiences for which it has not had a chance to prepare itself. The spiritual journey, hard and arduous, puts wear and tear upon our physical selves. In the past, many saints attempted the journey with no concern for the body either. Many literally burnt out before their time.

An integrative spirituality will neither neglect nor despise the body, for the body also is capable of being a revelatory instrument. And properly fitted out, the body can serve as a great vehicle for the journey. Our meditation prepares the body for this journey. But when we constantly abuse the body, shocking it and disregarding its needs and health, we engage in a process that may not only open us to fantastic insights and experiences but may also prove one-sided and even destructive.

Balanced people grow on all three levels. It's too easy and very tempting for us to concentrate upon an aspect of our being that we already have some competence and control over. But in reality, the muscular jock with no brains and no depth of spirit is as pathetic as the superficial egghead whose knowledge bears no relation to his life and whose body is incapable of supporting a brain that size.

• The second rule is that the results of the spiritual work provide a means of discernment. "By their fruits you shall know them." Does this work have some real effect in our lives? We all go through times when we're not productive. At times all I seem to be giving forth is anger, frustration, and tension. These are times that must come during the spiritual journey. This work is difficult and not without pain, frustration, mistakes, and actual sins or hurting others. But our life in general outside these painful periods should show some fruits of this work—concrete incidents that indicate we're changing and growing as human beings and loving people.

The Jewish and Christian traditions don't allow for a real spirituality divorced from the life of the world. Christian monasticism can never involve rejection of the world. The monk's prayer must be concerned with the world; if it isn't, then he is stuck in his own egotism. To become like God means to open oneself in love to the world.

Let's look for the fruits in our own lives. We should judge our meditation or body work on not just itself. Building a good body is not the ultimate goal, and neither is a meditation without distractions. This work is a leaven for the rest of our lives. If our meditation doesn't help us love our neighbors more, open our generosity to our friends, or enable us to feel true compassion for the suffering, our spirituality is dead. Here is a list of fruits, given by the apostle Paul: the harvest of the Spirit is love, joy, peace, patience, kindness, goodness, fidelity, gentleness, and self-control. This list is not exhaustive. Nor is it a law. And it is certainly not peculiar to Christianity. Paul got it from

82

the Stoics, and a Buddhist list would be much the same. But like all such lists, it points us in the right direction. It shows us what the fruit we seek to harvest looks like.

When I was beginning the work of meditation, I would go—enthusiastic about my practice—to see my spiritual director. I wanted to make sure I was doing the right thing. He would listen to all I had to say. Then he would ask his question. And though the words differed from week to week, the essence remained the same: "And how are you getting along with the people you live with?" This is the acid test; our ordinary lives determine whether our meditation is spirituality or just a trippy experience that we use to escape from the real.

• The third rule of discernment involves openness to another person. The greatest insight into our own spiritual life often comes when we're able to reveal ourselves to another and then see ourselves reflected by that other person. I'm referring to the spiritual director, the teacher, the guru. Here is someone you believe is spiritual and also on the path, someone you feel you can open yourself to in dialogue. With this other person, you can put into words what you're experiencing.

We're not in an equal relationship with this director. Rather she or he evaluates and actually judges our spiritual lives. We have a tendency in spiritual work to stray from the path. Each spiritual tradition warns about ways in which we may become lost. Since it is such a delicate, deep, and personal work, the only way in which we can be sure we're not going around in circles or falling into some trap is to open ourselves courageously and allow our experiences to be tested by someone more experienced on this road than we are. The deceptions of others are much easier to spot than the deceptions we put on ourselves.

But aren't these gifted people few and far between? And how will I ever convince one of them to listen to me? First, we don't need a personal director at the beginning of this work. We can do a great deal on our own. When the time comes, most spiritual traditions promise that our director will appear. Chances are that he or she will not carry a big sign saying, "I am a spiritual director." It might be your Polish grandmother who never had much schooling in her life but who—when it comes to living—knows more than a whole university of professors put together. In a spiritual director, we're looking for someone who knows how to live and can guide us along that same path.

We can also evaluate our journey with an object. There are a number of tools for spiritual exploration available today in our culture—the I Ching, Tarot cards, and astrology. Unfortunately we have regarded these as primitive and superstitious means of fortune telling, and they have been so perverted. But in their uncorrupt forms, they are no more fortune-telling devices than the Old Testament prophets were engaged in telling the future. These are tools of psychic and spiritual exploration. They throw a beam of light into the darkness of our psyche, providing hints and clues to the processes at work in our depths.

The I Ching is an ancient Chinese book of oracles, which took form slowly over the centuries. To put its philosophy very simply, the I Ching says that in the midst of this changing world there is a way to go beneath the changes and perceive the patterns of change. Or we might go above all the little changes we're in the midst of, and then from this loftier vantage point, we can perceive the pattern in all the small changes. But then isn't the I Ching talking about the spirit? For the spirit of God is always the same, above all change yesterday, today, and tomorrow. As a tool, the I Ching helps us perceive the spirit in a particular event.

Of course the temptation is to fall into divination rather than spirituality. To avoid this trap, let's use the I Ching or one of these other tools in prayer and not put specific questions to it at the start. The oracle of the I Ching speaks to the particular moment in which we are present. Thus we can consult it for a hint at the direction of the present moment. It speaks, not with a cut-and-dried answer, but through a delicate shimmering language of images that provides a lure and hook by which we may fish in our psyche with the hope of catching a glimpse of the movements of our spirit. We accomplish this through a meditation upon whatever oracle our throw of the coins leads us to. We look not for specific things (although sometimes the oracle is surprisingly specific), but we look for ways of acting, ways of being; we look for our inner wisdom to guide us as it speaks to us through the oracle.

Tarot cards may be used in much the same way. These cards embody powerful archetypes of the human unconscious—the king, the fool, the sun, justice, death, and so on. Choose a card at random, and spend your meditation with that card. Let it speak. Perhaps it will tell you a story about itself. Free-associate with the different objects and symbols on the card. Allow the images on the card to create vibrations deep within you. Let the card be like a dream. Don't look for clear ideas that you will immediately grasp the meaning of. Let your inner wisdom speak its own dark language; in time you will understand what it is saying. But it takes time and openness.

Of all these tools, astrology has been the most corrupted and bastardized. True astrology has nothing to do with what we find in the morning papers. I'm not suggesting you try the kind of astrology that tells us what to do. But real astrology provides a map that can throw light upon the inner self. It can bring aspects of our spirit into the light of knowledge. It is not *the* map; there is no single magical map. But it is one way of knowledge. And a horoscope properly drawn up and interpreted can provide much food for meditation and enable us to know ourselves better. Astrology is a tool for growth rather than a crutch for living, or worse yet a deceptive magic. These tools have nourished humanity throughout the ages. They provide a handle on what is happening in our lives.

III

THE EXPERIENCE OF PRAYER

Eleven

Music and Art

Art and music can be beautiful forms of prayer as well as vehicles to prayer. Like prayer, art and music stretch our imagination. And unless we're gifted with an artistic flair, we tend to be rather unimaginative by nature. But if we're ever to see the kingdom of God, our pedestrian imaginations must be stretched to receive a vision so grand. Music and art expand our limited horizons; musicians and artists are gifted in the realm of imagination; they see and hear beauty that we fail to notice until it's pointed out.

My own passion for music began during high school. For me, as a rather shy and secluded teen-ager, the world of opera became in a real sense my own world; in this dream world of love and death, I lived vicariously. Granted that growing up vicariously is not the ideal, but without music, I might have been even more isolated from the world of human and emotional contact. Here was a world of beauty and life that I loved and could feel at home in.

Music, and dramatic music in particular, soon led me to a different kind of drama. One night I heard a performance of Verdi's *Requiem*. Verdi had taken the Catholic service for the dead and transformed it into opera. Here were all the terrors of the Day of Judgment, and all the emotions with which we'd face such a day—the fear, the trembling, the pleading to be spared. But this was not just another opera—not just another romantic story. Some people believed this story was true—it was part of a religion.

Many years later, I entered this faith because of the beauty of its stories (not necessarily the Last Judgment) and because throughout the years, this faith had nourished and encouraged her musicians and artists to retell the stories through their own imaginative powers. I had lived for music and art, and now I found a church that loved them as I did. I had found a home and a family.

I specifically mention music because that has been my own way into the inner life. But the same journey can be made through the visual arts or through literature. Each of us has some pathway into the realm of inner experience; the arts unfold that realm for us and transport us there more easily than any other vehicle.

But how can music and art create a prayer experience? Let's begin with music since we have already been talking about it. Music frees us from the whole trap we create for ourselves with words. Now words are by no means evil. Through the art of speaking, we differentiate ourselves from all other animals. Words are the primary tools in the creation of our humanity, but they also limit us. Words dominate our lives. They constantly flow through our minds. Their noise keeps us from experiencing the silence of our own inner beings. When we sit to meditate, the noise we must battle most is the noise of words.

But there are other ways of communicating. We can communicate through our bodies, as when we touch or smile. Pure music communicates without the use of words, yet it speaks powerfully. Music frees us from words and from their limitations. Listening to music, we know something is being communicated to us, but we can't say exactly what is being shared. From the vantage point of words and concepts, we could say that the music is not specific. But our inability to describe a musical experience in words does not mean there is not communication. Communication need not be specific, or include clear boundaries, or be able to be articulated in words. And in music, we can sense different levels of communication. Some music speaks to me more powerfully than other music. The factor responsible is sympathy: I feel a real communion with that music that vibrates along the same levels as my own being. It speaks to me as other music does not.

The arts deal with subjective experiences. There are no objective criteria to evaluate an artistic work. Why does a certain melody seize us and sing in our hearts for days? We're being addressed on a level far deeper than words. Music frees us from our entrapment by words.

Music not only bypasses words but it also avoids concepts and ideas. People complain they can't appreciate and understand abstract art. Yet music is entirely abstract, and few people ever bemoan its abstractness. In fact, music is closer to mathematics than to the visual arts. Like mathematics, it totally transcends words. When we enjoy a piece of pure music, we're in the realm of pure form.

Even when music is joined to words, the music adds a depth and power that the words alone could never manage. The words launch the music; they focus our attention and provide the music with a more precise reference to our articulated world. But the music swiftly leaves the words behind as it probes emotional and spiritual contents more directly than is possible with words. Consider the phenomenon of opera in America today. It seems absurd to perform opera in a language the audience does not understand. Yet opera communicates and is a popular art form today because it does communicate—not through the words, but through the music.

The Visual Arts

On the other hand, the visual arts use our most literal sense—sight— and open up the possibilities of flying beyond the literal into new realms of seeing. I find myself very much confined to the literal when it comes to vision. I remember as a child thinking that drawings and paintings were only a primitive attempt to do what photography could do with much more fidelity. The painting of a landscape was, in my view, inferior to a color photo of that same scene. It was a revelation to me when I first realized the artist might not want merely to reproduce what is visible to the naked eye but rather might wish to paint what she or he saw through imagination. Then I realized that other people imagined through their sight the way I did through music and words. The sense of sight could be as open to the fantastic and ideal as the sense of sound or language.

Although I have no talent in the visual arts and barely more insight and appreciation, yet my contacts with the visual arts have been of immense help and importance in my own human growth. Unlike my approach to music or words, I don't come to the visual arts with natural gifts and talents. But despite my natural blindness in this sphere, possible ways of seeing the world have been revealed and opened up to me. I now know that even what I consider bare ordinary reality is colored by my own imagination or lack of it. And once I've come to recognize my imagination at work shaping my world, then I'm able to let that imagination develop and become more creative in my life.

We don't have to allow any of our five senses to be cut off from the creative power of the imagination. The visual arts, in spite of their arising from very concrete objects in our world, are fully as imaginative as music. Nothing in our world of perception need be permanently bound merely to the representation of what is. Any object may come alive if it is seen through the creative touch of imagination.

The Powers of Imagination

Many people are gifted with imagination in only one or two areas of life. We are blind and prosaic in the other realms and senses. The practice of prayer can help us most in these areas of blindness. In college, the one art-history course I took taught me more than any other course, if only because I walked into it knowing least about the subject. It opened for me a new world. Other classes merely explored worlds I was already acquainted with. Perhaps I will never come to understand and celebrate the visual arts in a way equal to others, but my eyes have been opened; I have seen what visual imagination looks like. When it is pointed out to me or when it knocks me over with its beauty, I can appreciate it. And I can also begin to see what part visual imagination can play in my own life.

Whatever opens me further to the beauty of the world, to the divine spark that dwells deep down within each creature—whatever brings me to this awareness is truly prayer.

In my encounter with the visual arts, I began my appreciation in the wild world of fantasy and surrealism. I could only recognize the visual imagination at work when it was a full-blown creation of airy castles. But as I deepened my encounter with art, I saw that the power of imagination was not a work merely in the fantastic. The greatest artists transformed the mundane and ordinary. They saw and communicated in a flower, a look, a human figure, something more than the ordinary. They perceived in the flower something alive, something with the spark of life that if we too might recognize it, we might call God.

Our imagination can be divorced from reality, and when this is so, it has a wondrous magical shimmering quality of its own. We need fantasy and escape if only as a Sabbath rest from the pain of existence. But the fantastic is not the apex of the imagination, even if it is imagination at its most theatrical and dazzling brilliance. And if we recognize imagination only in the fantastic, then imagination—divorced from the rest of our lives—becomes an escape—unreal and a narcotic.

We must also discover imagination in our everyday lives. It can play a role in the way we see ordinary objects, events, and people—a leaf, a parade, a smile. Here the great artists have sought to discern the spark of God, and when they were able, they have communicated this spark to those of us less gifted in the power of sight. Art opens our eyes to the presence of the divine in our ordinary day. It calls us to discover what is true, good, and beautiful in our own lives from day to day. And when our eyes have seen the glory, then we appreciate it, celebrate it, and worship it.

Art opens me to what the world could be, revealing possibilities dormant within the present. William Blake, the poet and painter, was once on a hill with a friend at sunrise. As the sun rose, Blake turned to his friend to ask what he saw. "Why, I see the great sun rising in the sky. What do you see?"

"I see the choirs of angels in heaven singing, 'Glory to God in the highest,' " replied Blake. It takes the artist to see a vision in what we dismiss and forget as we see merely a great ball of fire. But the artist sees the sun for what it truly is—the Creation showing the glory of the Creator. And great art opens us to that religious experience.

Music and art in their different ways form bridges between what is spiritual—the kingdom of God—and what is mundane—our world. Music works with the ideal: it operates on the level of pure mathematics. But through music, this lofty ideal communicates directly to us. We are moved and transformed without any intervening concept or word. And this process is the very process we seek in our own ordinary meditation. In meditation we practice perceiving directly without any intervention of mind or word. We practice working around all the concepts, ideas, and constructs that distort and interfere with our direct perception of the world. The meditation allows us to perceive the world directly rather than filtered through what we think the world really is. Such an experience is very hard to attain, but through music we can catch a glimpse.

Art, on the other hand, moves from this world up. Whereas music begins in the ideal world of perfect forms, art begins with the world of sense and allows it to become transparent to the divine. Only when music is tied to words or to a program does it take on a concrete worldly shape. And art, when it is abstract, assumes some of music's characteristics. But otherwise it is tied into the familiar world we see. Yet real art never leaves us in that matter-of-fact world. It explores the hidden dimensions of that world; it lifts us into the same realm as music—the realm of the spirit. But in art, it is a spirit, not as it is in itself in some perfect form, but rather the spirit as it is incarnated and enfleshed in our world, the world of the senses.

Praying with Art and Music

The most obvious way to pray through art and music is to listen to music and look at art. Allow the experience to happen to you—to take you up into the artist's vision so that you share his or her way of seeing the world. And then you can be thankful for sharing such an experience.

But there is a more prayerful way of coming into contact with the arts than the average concert or gallery experience provides. Let's first pray with music, since most of us have access at home to a stereo system. Decide on a piece of music you especially like. It doesn't have to be sacred, but it should be a rather quiet piece and should be pure music (no words). Now lie down on a couch or bed and take about five to ten minutes to relax fully. You might use the process of tension and relaxation described before (page 75).

When you're relaxed, begin playing the music at a fairly low volume so that it will not break the mood. (Often I like to use earphones because they provide a wonderfully close experience of the music.) Now let the music transport you wherever it wants. Close your eyes and let in whatever images and ideas want to enter your consciousness. Let the music conjure up a waking dream. Don't search for images; relax and wait, and they'll come. Also don't look for the meaning of what is happening. When we use this technique, the music helps us pray; it opens us up and takes us places. And we shouldn't be concerned about going to the right place. Let's not wonder what the composer had in mind; let's be concerned rather to surrender to the music's message to us.

We can use the visual arts in much the same way. Of course great art is locked up in museums, so we don't have the control over the environment that we do with music in the privacy of our own homes. But most museums are also conducive in atmosphere to the relaxed meditative state of consciousness. The difference between our prayer tour of the museum and a normal tour is that now we will look at only very few works of art. We'll let one or two works we love speak to us.

Let's begin by finding a seat and sitting down for a few minutes. Take a few deep breaths and relax your body. Then spend some time with your eyes closed, observing your breath as it enters and leaves your body. When you feel sufficiently relaxed and receptive, move to the art object you would like to pray with. Begin by simply being with the art. Then perhaps you will want to go sit down again, close your eyes, and allow images to come up called forth by the art. The important element in this meditation is time: don't rush. Allow yourself and the art enough time to communicate fully and speak to one another.

In both these prayer experiences—music and art—you'll want to jot down what happens in your journal before you begin to forget it. This material should be entered into the prayer-experience section. And don't feel limited to words. Perhaps the music will speak in images of sight or smell. The art may speak in music or story.

But the journal keeping here is important for a number of reasons. First, it forces you to be aware of what's occurring. Often you can drift off into reverie, but you don't want to do that now: you're engaged now in the work of prayer, which demands that you should be relaxed. But it also demands that you should be awake and attentive to what is happening. The journal calls you to your work.

Second, the process of working in the journal acts as a catalyst for further prayer experiences. The act of writing or drawing can trigger other ideas and experiences, which expand through their being recorded. Finally the journal, in the prayer-gifts section, provides a treasury of prayer experiences that you may wish to relive and reexperience later.

At the beginning of this prayer experience, you may be very critical and skeptical of yourself. Images may arise in our consciousness, but we dismiss them as mere daydreaming: we don't consider them significant. But once again, we should remember not to judge our prayer experience. Let's accept and rejoice in each prayer for just what it is. These images come from my inner self, and therefore they can never be superficial or unimportant to me.

The best way to pray with art and music is to enter into the creative process itself, if we have either the talent or the inclination. And the crucial question here is not whether we're talented but whether what we do in art and music enables us to transcend ourselves and rejoice in our extended vision.

Modern society has practically put the amateur out of business.

Who wants to hear the local pianist perform Beethoven when we can buy records and listen to any number of professionals perform it? Amateurism has gone into retreat. But the amateur has always had a place in the arts, not in competition with the professional, but alongside. The amateur composes, plays, and draws simply out of the love of doing it. And in the process of being involved in the creation of art, we can be opened to God because we ourselves experience the love that expressed itself in the creation of the world. Whether we draw poorly or well is not the point. The point is that we, from our limited viewpoint, put our own way of seeing onto canvas. And in that act of creation, we are for a moment like God.

I took piano lessons for fifteen years as I grew up. I learned to use the piano to dissipate and discharge my anger. When I became angry, depressed, or filled with joy, playing the piano brought these feelings into the open, where they could be released and celebrated. And at least with the destructive feelings, this method of release was better and more enjoyable than punching pillows or playmates. After banging the piano for a couple of hours, I would experience a transformation of emotions. The anger would disappear, and I would find peace. Music-making had removed the anger and replaced it with serenity. My becoming one with the music had healed me and restored me to peace.

In some way then, let us enter into the experience of God the Creator. Take some modeling clay and go to work. Throughout Jewish and Christian tradition, God is spoken of as the sculptor or the potter. Through our work in clay, we experience God as he creates the world through love. All it takes is getting our hands dirty and letting our imagination free. Besides, it's fun.

Twelve

The Prayer of Sports

Sports as a prayer experience may sound like a strange idea. But prayer may develop out of work on the body. When the body work ceases being an exercise and becomes an experience of transcendence, it becomes prayer. But there are many problems that militate against sports as prayer and prevent sport from becoming prayerful for us. Our personal experience with sport has probably been far from a prayer experience. Despite the corruption of sport, the experience as prayer lives on (even though people who experience sport in this way don't normally use the word prayer to describe it).

Obstacles to Sports Prayer

Professionalism debilitates sport as prayer. We're a nation of sports watchers rather than players. Sport is the domain of the professional, and the rest of us generally enter into the game only vicariously. Most of humanity is excepted from participation. As I was growing up (and I typified the nonathletic in the extreme), I never wanted to be a sportsman, and under the pretext that I had no talent or abilities, I generalized to never wanting to take part in any physical activity. Since I could not do certain things naturally, such as catch a ball or throw overhand, I assumed I was unfit for sports and grew up feeling fear and loathing every time I was forced to take part in sports. My field was the intellect, not left field, where all too often someone hit the ball and embarrassed me.

But professionalism, although very ancient, is not the original understanding of sport in Western civilization. The Olympic Games have enshrined our ideal of the physical dimension of life for millennia, and they began as a celebration of the human bodily potential.

95

The physical ideal was considered a part of being a total human being. The Olympics, at least at their birth, were a celebration of ordinary human beings working on their physical bodies and shaping them to perfection. How many of us today, especially if we are over thirty, feel any real call to celebrate life through our physical prowess?

When sports became professional, they turned from an avocation into a vocation, from an entertainment into a business. We relate to sport as spectators just as we relate to music and art as enjoyers but not as creators. And the sports our culture values make us spectators. Very few people in their right mind are going to engage in football regularly after they reach a certain age: only the young can play with the necessary stamina and pliability of the body. Yet football is the American sport, even though it's restricted to the select few.

Yet we do not need to leave the life of the body to the professionals. Every one of us has a body. A whole world of experience lies in its exploration. We can do something with our bodies besides letting them run down; we can perfect them and bring them alive. Sports are not just for sportspeople.

Competition is another disease that prevents sport from being prayer. As in many other activities (meditation included, until we break the habit), the goal in sports is the only thing that counts. The major consideration is who wins and loses rather than the process of the game itself and the opportunities for ecstasy in the play. So the idea of competition and all the negative feelings and emotions it raises make the environment unfit for prayer.

And even when we move out of the arena of sports themselves to deal with physical fitness, we still run into serious problems that prevent prayer from happening. When I grew up, calisthenics were a drudge, but you put up with them so that you could be in decent shape. Now I for one early on opted out of being in decent shape and so had no use for calisthenics. But late in life, when I realized my body wasn't going to last forever and that unless it was exercised, it wouldn't even last as long as it should, then I began doing calisthenics as a kind of insurance policy. But such a view is very shortsighted and misses the entire transcendent experience that can be created through body work. Sports have also suffered because of the separation, dominant for so long in Western experience, of the spirit, the mind, and the body. These ideals have grown up separate in the West; seldom have we stressed that they be part of the same person. Instead, we have encouraged and even expected people to excel in just one of these areas, ending up with the stereotypes of the jock, the egghead, and the monk. The monk is not smart and does not play sports except in cute films where Sister Joseph Marie shows she can hit a home run.

Sports as Prayer

Now, having considered all these problems that plague the great notion of sport, let us nevertheless try to view sport as a prayer and as a spiritual discipline. We begin with a question to the sportsperson, since I assume most of us here are not really at ease with our bodies. This question has been with me a long time, but before now, I have felt it too dumb to ask: "What does the athlete get out of the sport?"

Obviously the athlete enjoys the sport: there is the thrill of competition and of victory. But there must be something more to impel people to put all the time, struggle, and pain into sports necessary to excel. But until recently, no one else bothered to ask the athlete this question. Nor did the sportsperson deal with the question (after all athletes are not supposed to be interested in theories but only in practice). Yet as the question began to be asked, sportspeople tried to articulate what it was in sport that satisfied. The answers went far beyond competition and victory. In the midst of sports, these people experienced a union of all aspects of their being; they felt in touch with more than themselves, or they talked of the game actually playing itself: they were part of that whole and didn't feel they were playing the game but rather that the game was playing them. For example, in professional football, there are a number of cases that in the old days we would simply chalk down to luck, but what really is happening is a kind of precognition. In the midst of the action, something occurs so that a player lunges at another player before the ball has even been thrown. A response has taken place before the occurrence of the event that should normally elicit the response. And if the person can talk about this instance, he may say something like, "Well, suddenly everything was clear. I could see the energy, and I knew what was going to happen." Or they may talk about the game in terms of slow motion—that at a certain point in the game, time slowed down and there seemed to be all the time in the world to do what they had to do. Their part in the game was to let the event happen.

Such talk fits in with mystical experience better than with football, but perhaps our understanding of football is too narrow. The experience is there, and we can witness its results in these "lucky" plays. Besides, who would ever think of looking for mystical experiences in football? Not the mystic, not the footballer, and least of all the fan. So no one considers whether there is indeed a form of spiritual experience here.

When we enter into the world of the sport, when we have forgotten ourselves, when our ego has gone to sleep, we become part of a larger whole. *Zen in the Art of Archery* dared deal with sports in terms of mysticism. At the time (now of course it has become a classic), it appeared to be a very strange book. Today of course such titles abound, and we even have *Zen and the Art of Motorcycle Maintenance*. But what does spirituality have to do with learning how to shoot an arrow? Everything. To learn to shoot an arrow well, we must give up the conscious control we exert over our movements. We have to relinquish the mind to the spirit and the body. And when we can let go of the shooting by the mind, then the arrow shoots us or it shoots itself. When we begin to think about such an action, the mind actually gets in the way and trips us up.

Walking with Awareness

We can experience this phenomenon ourselves. Really think about walking some time. Consider in your mind each movement before you allow it to happen. Chances are you'll either stumble or be wobbly before you have taken ten steps. But if you allow the body to walk itself, it will do an expert job with almost no help from the mind at all, avoiding obstacles that could trip or throw you off balance.

Tennis and Golf

Tennis and golf provide the same kind of experience as archery—the experience of the ball hitting itself. When we put all of our conscious energy into trying to put the ball where we want it, we're liable to miss. But if we acquire enough skill to let go, allowing the club or racket to play itself, then we, the racket, and the ball become one instead of three separate things. From this oneness comes not only a beautiful putt or volley but also that wonderful feeling of ecstasy.

Earlier we noted the same concept at work in the film *Star Wars*. Luke is able to deliver the missile into the tiny corridor, not because of his senses or his computers, but because he allows the Force to work through him, and in a sense, he becomes one with the entire event.

Tai Chi and Mountain Climbing

When we become one with the sports event, we're participating in the harmony of the world. The Chinese concept of *yin* and *yang* represents all the opposites in the world that actually complement and relate to one another, such as masculine and feminine, night and day, light and dark, good and evil. The world of sport provides an entrance into this flow. Aikido, the Japanese art of self-defense, allows the adept to stand very much at peace and at ease. When the attacker comes to throw himself at the person, immediately the attacker is on the floor while the practitioner of Aikido—with no effort and almost no movement—is still standing quietly. She has used no force of her own whatsoever.

Well, how does she overthrow her aggressor? By entering into the harmony of the situation, she uses the attacker's energy and allows that energy to work through to its natural conclusion. However, she deflects that energy away from herself. She does not oppose it; that would take immense energy and force of her own. Instead, she deflects it a little and allows it to run its course. So the attacker bounds into the mat rather than his intended target. And this art is not gained through the use of force but in seeing and then using the rhythm that already exists in the situation.

The gentle Chinese system of Tai Chi looks more like a dance than a martial art. The person is playing with the energies around him. Of course to the uninitiated and to the beginner, it looks as though the play is with empty air. But after a while, if you open yourself to the experience, if you allow the experience to manifest itself to you instead of making a judgment that such experience is only illusory or impossible, then you can tune in to these subtle energies and experience the energy flow around and through you.

Or let us consider long-distance running—one of the most demanding and excruciating sports. Why would people want to put their bodies through this grueling workout? In running, when you reach the stage where it seems as though the body is at the breaking point, you can—by pressing just a little farther—break through into the beyond. And then running is the whole world, and the world is running.

Mountain climbing embodies the same experience. Why else would mountains be so important in religious imagery and stories? Moses receives the Ten Commandments on top of Mount Sinai, Elijah communes with God on Mount Carmel, Jesus delivers his sermon from the top of a mountain, he experiences his agony on the Mount of Olives, he dies on Mount Golgotha, and he ascends to heaven from still another mountain. Mountains transcend. By climbing, we surpass ourselves. We can do more than we ordinarily believe we're capable of. We don't have to live on level ground forever.

Not all movement prayer is sport. Dance also has been a part of the prayer life of many cultures, including our own. Perhaps the most famous instance of religious dancing is the whirling dervishes. But King David danced before the ark of the Lord. John the Baptist danced in his mother's womb when in the presence of Jesus. And dancing has had part in Christian worship, even though it has not been obviously present.

Dance

Let us try a movement exercise that has some qualities of the dance. It is called the routine of the sun and comes from the Hatha Yoga tradition. To do this movement, you will need some free floor space, which you will want to cover with a cloth or mat. You need enough room on the floor to stretch out from head to toe. This exercise involves bodily movements, breathing, and finally—if you're interested—the words of the Lord's Prayer in the mind. In learning the exercise, it is best to begin simply with the movements, then add the breathing, and finally the words, which are only thought, not said.

1. Stand up straight with your arms at your sides. *Breathing in* slowly, raise your arms until the palms join together with the arms stretched out over the head. *Breathing out*, bring the arms down so that the palms are joined in a prayer position, second and third fingers almost touching your chin. Prayer: Our Father. *Breathing in*, interlock the two thumbs and separate the hands so that both palms of the interlocked hands are pointed away from you. Now stretch the arms up again, keeping the thumbs locked. Prayer: Who Art In Heaven. Continue this stretching movement backward so that you are bending backward, arms stretched into the air. Hold this stretch for a moment. During this movement, keep your eyes on your thumbs at all times.

2. *Breathe out*, and bend the whole body forward so that the head bends down toward and touches the knees. The hands now should rest palms down on the floor to either side of the feet, with the tips of your fingers and toes on a straight line. The knees must not bend in this process. Throughout the entire exercise, stretch only as far as you can with comfort. With practice, your body will become more supple and will be able to accommodate each movement. If now you cannot touch

the floor with your palms without bending the knees, then bend the knees in order to place your palms on the floor. Prayer: Hallowed Be Thy Name.

3. *Breathing in*, stretch back your right leg as far back as you can, and allow the knee to drop to the floor. In this position, continue the stretch by looking up to the ceiling and back as far as you can—this stretches the entire spine. Prayer: Thy Kingdom Come.

4. *Breathing out*, stretch the left leg back to join the right. Both feet rest only on the toes. Now push the body up into a position in which only the toes and palms are on the floor. This position is familiar from the push-up. The torso should be relatively straight in this position. Prayer: Thy Will Be Done.

5. *Breathing in*, lower first the knees (Prayer: On Earth), then the chin (As It Is), and finally the chest (In Heaven) to the floor. At the conclusion, the body is touching the floor with only the toes and palms and these three points. The stomach is still slightly off the floor. The secret to achieving this position lies in never moving the palms from where they are placed in step 2 and in keeping the feet where they are placed in steps 3 and 4.

6. *Holding the breath*, push yourself up into what is called the cobra pose. Here, using the palms for leverage, you first raise and bend back the head as you lift it off the mat and then follow through with the rest of the upper back. Thus you are lifting your head and back off the mat and bending them backward. Use your eyes as a lever. Look up as far as you can and look backward as far as you can. You should feel this stretch in your neck and all down the spine. During the stretch, your stomach, thighs, palms, and feet should not leave the floor. The legs and feet should remain touching. There will be a tendency for them to separate. Going into the stretch, imagine each vertebra of your spine lifting off the mat separately. Prayer: Give Us This Day Our Daily Bread.

7. *Breathing out*, push your body up into a triangle so that only the palms and toes are on the floor and your behind sticks up in the air. Your head should be right between your two arms so that it does not stick out. In this position, feel the stretch in your legs. Try to touch

the heels to the ground. Prayer: And Forgive Us Our Trespasses.

8. *Breathing in,* bring the right foot up to its former position between your palms. Let the left knee sink to the floor. This is the same position as step 3, only reversed. Prayer: As We Forgive Those Who Trespass against Us.

9. *Breathing out,* bring the left foot up to join the right. You are now again in the same position as at the end of step 2. Prayer: And Lead Us Not into Temptation.

10. *Breathing in,* stretch the body up, thumbs locked, and keep the movement going until the body is stretched out with hands extended above the head. Continue the stretch backward as in step 1. Prayer: But Deliver Us from Evil.

11. *Breathing out,* bring the arms forward, join the palms together in the praying gesture, and touch the thumbs to the forehead (Prayer: For Thine Is the Kingdom), the mouth (and the Power), and the heart (and the Glory) and let the hands fall to the sides (Forever and Ever. Amen). Close your eyes and rest a moment.

This movement seems complex at first. But with a little practice, it becomes an easy and beautiful way to begin the day. It is good to practice it three or four times a day—for not only the stretching but also the relaxation and the prayer.

Guidelines for Praying in Sports

First of all, if sport is to be prayerful, set competiton at a low priority. Competition is not bad; it adds spice and zest to the sport. But when competition dominates, as it so often does today, then the whole sport begins to focus on the outcome rather than on the activity itself. Gaining popularity today are sports such as tennis and golf where the competition aspect does not always dominate over the exaltation of simply playing.

The second guideline has to do with penetrating into that realm beyond conscious action. One of my initial problems with sports was that no one bothered to tell me that I could work at becoming adept in my body. I assumed I was not cut out for bodily activity, and I left such activity to those who were talented. Since sports were supposed to be fun and recreational, I thought they shouldn't need to be learned or practiced. God knows where I would have gotten with the same attitude about piano playing. Sports *are* recreational, but in order to enjoy them fully, we must become proficient in them. As long as we are still at the stage where we're *consciously* playing tennis, we're recreating, but that sport isn't yet a vehicle for release and transcendence.

Sport, like any other spiritual activity, needs practice and proficiency. And the true prayer experiences of sport won't be ours until we've broken through into the realm of unity, where there is no longer the player and the game but rather a unified whole. If we wish to undertake sports as a spiritual discipline, or even as a great recreation, we must commit ourselves to persevere until we reach this plateau. And it is possible to reach it. Sports are not just the domain of the professional. Indeed, like music, art, and poetry, it is truly the domain of the amateur—the person who does it for love rather than for a living.

The final guideline is to seek fun, fulfillment, and wholeness. Let's drop this utilitarian idea that we exercise as some bodily insurance so that we'll live longer. This utilitarian concept, whether it applies to sports, to prayer, or to life, is a very poor excuse for anything. If we are going to be one with the body, then for our own sakes, let's find some activity that we really want to do because we believe we will enjoy doing it. There are certainly enough different and various possibilities to choose from.

If you do not enjoy being matched against other people in a game, then choose something such as jogging. If you value grace over strenuous exercise, choose Tai Chi or dancing. If you're afraid and would like to build up confidence in your ability to defend yourself, choose Aikido or another martial art. If you don't like the outdoors, avoid golf. If you wish a more explicit spiritual dimension, try Yoga, Kum Nye, or perhaps Sufi whirling. And finally, if you don't feel any real desire to work with the body, then go on to something else. The time will come at its own appropriate moment.

Sports can be prayerful, they can expand our awareness of the world, they can be a celebration of being alive. This experience of prayer is possible for each one of us. Indeed, of all the forms of spirituality discussed in this book, sports is the most direct and provides easiest entrance into this new dimension of being alive.

Thirteen

Prayer as a Nature Walk

It might seem as though prayer with nature actually could fit into one of the other prayer experiences we have already discussed. Prayer with nature might be considered a combination of the prayer styles explored in music, art, and sport. Yet if there is nothing new in the style and manner of our prayer here, still the object of this experience is unique and worthy of our attention. Whereas in art and music we pray through the imagination of humanity, in nature we experience the art and music of God.

As an introduction to prayer in nature, let's consider a special kind of meditation that involves walking. It might at first seem paradoxical that we should consider walking a form of meditation. For we usually associate meditation with finding a very quiet place, sitting down, remaining still, and closing our eyes to shut out any outside distractions. How can walking, which involves constant movement and stimulation (both aural and visual), be akin to meditation?

Walking Meditation

We have difficulty with walking as meditation only if our ideas of meditation are narrow and limited. Although we usually must learn to meditate through a rather structured form, and with the environment and ourselves controlled as carefully as possible, still this is only a practice that prepares us to be capable of meditating throughout our waking day. Meditation is the process of being fully open to what is happening in our world. This process can occur anywhere. It need not be restricted to only those times we set aside for formal meditation. In fact, if we restrict the meditative experience to just those times, we're losing much of the fruit that can come from meditation.

The image of leaven or yeast in bread can serve as an image for meditation in our life. The yeast is not the bread. But if the yeast is missing, the bread never rises, remaining just a lump of dough. The yeast is indispensable, but it is not present for its own sake: it enables the bread to rise. It is the same with meditation. In the prayer of walking, we begin to lead our meditation experience out of its special niche and allow it to flow over into our waking life.

First find a quiet natural place where you want to walk—someplace rather secluded so you will not be distracted by people, and someplace where the walk is easy. This is not the time to climb mountains or clear paths through the wilderness. How about a nice walk through the woods, down the beach, along a meadow, or even down a country road? And you will also want to allow yourself plenty of time for the walk—perhaps a whole morning or afternoon.

Let's begin the nature walk with some sitting meditation. Find a comfortable spot, sit down for five or so minutes, and turn your attention toward your breathing. This can be your entry into the prayer experience. It is your gateway, your door at which you leave behind all the thoughts, anxieties, and tensions you have brought with you. Here is your metaphorical shower where you can clean yourself of all the psychic dirt and grime you've picked up, so you can enter into your walk with a new and clear being. We need such gateways into prayer because they provide time to rediscover ourselves and to find our center again.

When you're calm and clear, rise and begin your walk. But now you walk differently from the walking you do the rest of the day. Ordinary walking has some purpose. I usually walk with a vengeance. We walk not for the sake of walking but for the sake of getting somewhere. But your walk today has no place to go; the goal today is the walk itself. Here is one of those rare chances to do absolutely nothing. There is no goal ahead, no task to carry out, no time by which you must be finished. There is no competition with anyone else or even with yourself. You're free from limits. You shouldn't even decide now where your walk will take you or how far you'll try to go. You may take the whole time to walk half a mile, or you may cover ten miles. This will be determined by what happens as you walk, not by any previous expectations. Let the process determine where you go, how you go, and how far you go.

Since you have nothing at all to do and no set limit, you can take the time on this walk to allow something to happen. You have no expectations about what that might be. And you have no anxieties either. You'll simply allow what wants to happen to occur. And if nothing happens to you, then that is precious and valuable as well. There is no way you can fail, just as there is nothing called success here; there is only experience. You're merely setting out to walk.

Be Attentive to the Walk

And as we walk, we'll want to do our walking in a different way from usual. Let's come fully alive to our walking. First we might turn our attention to the process of walking itself.

For a few moments, walk very slowly. During that time, look down at your feet. See if you can feel each individual movement involved in taking a step. Feel how the weight of your body is supported on your left foot. Be aware of how your left foot rests on the ground. How does it support and balance your body? And be conscious of what's happening as your right foot swings in front of you to take the next step. What happens now to your left foot? Observe how the weight slowly shifts from the center of the foot toward the toe as the heel begins to leave the ground. Now your weight is centered on the toes. Be aware of when and how the right foot touches the ground. What part of the foot touches the ground first? Feel the shifting of the weight from the left to the right foot as it takes over support and balance.

Continue this very slow conscious walking for a few moments, all the while entering into the process of walking as fully as possible. You might become overly self-conscious and end up tripping or actually forgetting how to walk, but that's all right. The trick is to walk as normally as possible but to slow down the movement and to become aware of just how this walking is accomplished.

Feel where your balance is at each moment. Where is the center of your body? Are you centered in the best place for walking? You might want to experiment now by changing the center. As you walk along, put the center of your being first into your head: you're now very conscious of your mind and how it is programming, regulating, and observing the process of walking. Next put the center into your heart. Now your experience becomes more an experience of emotion and feeling. You're aware of how you're feeling during the walk: are you sad, joyful, at ease? Are you more aware of your environment when you're centered in the heart? How are you feeling about what is all around you?

Finally shift the center into that space a couple of inches below the navel. How do you experience the walking now? In this center, you might feel a unity with your environment. You might also feel a greater fluidity than in the other centers. For example, when we're centered in our minds, we often approach this experience in terms of analysis—what's happening at each separate moment. But when we're operating out of the body center, we tend to perceive walking as a flowing motion; we experience the whole rather than the individual parts. Take some time to experience these centers. At first they may sound very mysterious and even nonsensical. But with just a little experimentation and openness on your part, you can come to enrich your life through these three different centers of perception.

Opening the Senses

When we sat and meditated on our breaths, we experienced our senses, our bodies, and our spirits opening. We became aware of sounds that outside of meditation we had ignored and tuned out. And behind our closed eyelids, images rose into consciousness, becoming very vivid as our practice continued, and eventually becoming quite clear and powerful. And we became aware of our bodies and their experiences in ways that before would never rise into consciousness because our minds censored them as not worthy of our attention—bodily noises, itchings, and discomforts as well as feelings of well-being, rest, and peace. As we meditated we became aware of tensions that were present all the time but which were usually not painful enough to call attention to themselves. These were just a few of the ways our bodies opened during meditation on the breath.

Now as you walk with your eyes open, transfer your meditational experience into this new environment. Be aware of all there is to see. Open yourself to the particular sounds that strike your ears. Listen especially for those sounds that are soft or far away. Continue to be aware of your body as you continue to walk. Allow the body to be an integral part of the opening you're now enjoying. After all, here is a chance for your total being to be present to this unique moment with nature.

Just as in formal meditation you discovered your mind to be a major distraction with its chattering thoughts, so here, even though you have moved out of the traditional posture and routine, you should still be aware of and on guard against those distractions. You're not here to think thoughts about tomorrow, or about some conversation you had yesterday, or about any unfinished business that hangs over you. Rather you're here in this special environment to be fully present in the here and now. You have practiced being present in meditation; now you have the opportunity to bring that practice out into the rest of your life.

As we practice opening the senses, let's add another practice. We have spoken before about subtle energies. The spiritual traditions all talk about certain objects and places in nature as having good and bad energies. In the early part of Israel's history, her shrines were tied to manifestations of this nature energy: certain rocks, mountains, or rivers were considered sacred to God because of the energy felt in their presence.

Try to tune in to this subtle energy in the course of your walk. Pay particular attention to how a certain place, rock, or scene strikes you: can you feel a change in the energy here? Does a certain place strike you as very peaceful? Does another have a feeling of dread about it? Does one place seem very friendly, another rather cold and uninviting?

You'll sense these energies, not with your eyes only, but also with your whole being, and you'll sense it on a very subtle and deep level. In order to be able to sense it, you must be centered, and you must allow yourself to be open and receptive to very small stimuli. It takes practice, but that's what you're here for, isn't it?

Energy Fields

We need this prayer of nature because we live in cities filled with distractions and noise, far removed from the natural world that used to be the human environment. As we spoke before of fasting to purify and provide a vacation for our body, we might think of our day with nature as a sort of fast. Here is a chance to flush away many pollutions, problems, anxieties, and tensions that arise in our city environment to poison our spirit. The silence of the forest or the ocean can cleanse our hearing. Here, as opposed to the noise we ourselves create, are the natural sounds of earth: the rustling of the wind in the leaves, the pounding of waves on the shore, the songs of birds, the hot silence of an open meadow in August. During the other parts of our lives, we're in a terrible hurry, which also pollutes our spirit. Now we have an opportunity to give ourselves a rest—a change of pace. If we wish to stop, sit down, and let a particular scene enter into us, we have all the time we need right now. There is no agenda, nothing that we must do.

In our everyday lives, our eyes are under constant bombardment. But here we can rest our eyes. Let's allow our eyes to search out the world rather than have the world thrown at them, as often happens today in America. The objects of nature do not throw themselves at us; they simply are there, allowing themselves to be seen, but they won't force their presence upon us.

Work with a Camera

As we begin this prayer experience in nature, we might feel that we're out of our element. Perhaps we're not sure what this different kind of seeing is: we need some help, a tool perhaps. After all, we have learned to function rather well in all the hurry and the constant stimulation. We might feel rather lost in nature, experiencing boredom just because we're not comfortable relating to the world on such a peaceful and relaxed level. We don't know what to look for or listen to. The camera can help us see in this new meditative way.

> Take along a camera on your nature walk. Use it to search out scenes that open within you feelings of beauty, joy, awe, and stillness.

I have found in my own prayer experience that the camera helps overcome my blindness to the visual world. It has taught me that I see everything, not as it is, but through my own special perspective. I realize that what I do see implies whole other worlds that I don't see; by focusing my attention upon one thing, I at the same time withdraw attention from all the other possible objects in my world. Thus the camera points up my natural visual selectivity and then allows me to use my selective vision in a more creative and conscious way: I can really

109

choose what I shall look for in this walk. And whether I know it or not, I do indeed choose what I shall allow myself to see.

We use the camera not only to take pictures for future enjoyment. We are with the camera as part of the process of seeing. The taking of pictures is part of our meditation practice. Last summer I visited Mount Rainier in Washington. I took my camera along, my primary objective being a nice shot of the mountain. But the day was cloudy. When I got to the upper meadow, the mountaintop was still shrouded in the clouds. So I turned away from the mountain for a while and began to look around me. I was hunting for pictures of nature. Without my camera and my purpose of collecting pictures, I would not have been so observant. As I looked around for nature's objects of beauty, I first was drawn to the lovely small mountain wild flowers sprinkling the meadow.

And as I knelt to photograph the flowers, large drops of dew nestled all around the meadow grass caught my eye. Whenever the sunlight peeked through the clouds, the dew sparkled like jewels. I spent the next twenty minutes combing the meadow for the perfect picture of glistening dew. I'm not sure I ever really captured the experience on film. But that twenty-minute search was an experience of wonder and prayer that I probably never would have taken time for had I not been motivated by my camera.

Review of Our Experience

When you have finished your walk, sit down again for a few moments before you leave this prayerful place. Now enter into a more formal meditation. In the meditation, review what you have experienced in your walk today. Review what you experienced through your eyes, your sense of smell, your hearing, your touch, and your mind. And as you review your experience today, try to get in contact with feelings of thanksgiving and gratitude. These are the central emotions of prayer, and there are few experiences in our life better than contact with nature. It can wake within us this feeling of gratitude, of having been granted a priceless gift freely and with no strings attached.

Next you'll want to record your experience in your journal in the section on prayer experiences. If you have brought the journal with you on the walk, you can take the time to record your thoughts now. You do want to record your experience fairly soon after it occurs, before the process of forgetting sets in. Take some time to describe your experiences, thoughts, and feelings, using either an essay form or simply a series of notes.

Creation of the Haiku

Finally you want to take a prayer gift away from this experience, especially if you've found this walk good for you. A simple literary form is a suitable way to capture this prayer gift: it's the haiku. The haiku is a poem of three lines and seventeen syllables. The first line is seven syllables, and the second and third lines are five syllables each. The form will help you to refine your experience: it forces you to speak economically and with some power. In its own way it is a camera for the mind. Try it now, and remember that this too should have an element of prayer and play in it. When you are satisfied with your haiku, enter it in the prayer-gift section of the journal. You might actually write a number of haiku about your experience.

Here are a few haiku to help you with your inspiration:

> A riot of wind, dancing grass;
> the sun overhead
> ripens the meadow.

> The trees stretch their gaunt fingers
> to snare the pale moon
> and hoard her beauty.

> The still night hears the cricket
> and far off the rush
> of the whizzing cars.

> Pale pink sky, still breeze; and dew
> settling on the lawn;
> Nature's baptism.

Fourteen

Prayer as Story

Now we turn our attention to that peculiar human artifact, the world of words—and even more important, the worlds that words can create. Story as a product of human imagination is an almost universal gift. Many people have little or no aptitude for music, or for the visual arts, or for the body in sport. But practically everyone delights in telling and hearing stories, and we all tell stories. Some people, of course, are more gifted than others in the telling and creation of stories.

What is there about story that attracts us so? How does a story satisfy our very deeply felt needs and desires? Why is storytelling in one form or another the most popular form of human entertainment?

Story is able to create a whole new world. We are offered alternative ways of seeing and being in the world. We expand beyond our present limited experience and lifetime to participate in and embrace the total experience of not only the human race but also of the infinite number of possible universes as well.

But we should be clear just what we mean by story. It is first of all the stories we tell each other. And by extension, it is the literary story such as novel and drama. But story spills over into the other arts as well. We encounter it in the visual arts as film. It enters the musical arts as opera and song. The kinetic arts include dance, which tells story. And even competitive sport, which is limited in plot, includes a winner, a loser, and the progress of the game.

These story worlds offer a whole gestalt, a completeness rather than just an aspect of the totality. In music, by contrast, we do enter into another world, one completely dominated by the aural. Once entered, that world with its peculiar limitations is in itself whole, but it is not a fully human world. It is not our world, for it expands certain senses at the expense of others. And the same could be said for the visual and kinetic arts and for nature as well. But in the world of story, we enter into a particularly human world, which addresses us at all levels of our being.

Story and Religion

Story plays a vital part in humanity's life of prayer. First there are the stories that have been passed down from our own religious traditions. Religions arise when we ask questions such as where the world comes from, or why we are as we are, or what happens to us when we die. The first response to such questions comes, not in philosophy or theology, but as story.

In our own lives, such questions were first answered by stories. The question how we got here often takes the form of the stork who brings babies to mother and father. For a small child, this story provides more meaning than talking about sperm, eggs, fertilization, and pregnancy. As religion develops, it abstracts from these stories the material for philosophy, theology, and dogma. But before all of these "higher" forms of discourse exist, there is first the story providing a living perspective upon our own world. In story we have a vantage point from which we may view the world and our lives in it with meaning rathr than with confusion or outright chaos.

Jesus was renowned as a storyteller. He taught, not through philosophy or morals as did Aristotle, but through pointed parables—short fables concerning ordinary life. Story is at the center of Judaism as well—how Israel came to be, her birth in the waters of the Red Sea, the great heritage of the Law she received in the manifestation of God to Moses on the mountain of Sinai.

Stories That Teach

Stories, by taking us into a world and viewing that world from a particular vantage point, teach us in a more profound and satisfying manner than we could ever experience through abstract concepts and principles. Then, as we return from the storied world to our own, we bring with us that particular viewpoint, and we can look upon our own world from the new perspective.

One such story concerns the places and doctrines of heaven and hell, with which we're familiar. Yet this story in its simple way teaches us more than all the dogma.

Good man John dies, and since he was good, he soon appears before the heavenly gates. Saint Peter comes out to meet him there, welcomes him into the heavenly kingdom, and reveals that—since John had been so generous and kind—God has granted him one wish before entering heaven. John is rather taken aback by this. But after some consideration, he tells Saint Peter that he has been rather curious about what hell is like. Since, thank God, he is not going to spend eternity there, would it be possible for him to catch just a glimpse of hell before entering heaven? Saint Peter considers the request suitable and immediately escorts John to hell.

Entering hell, they come upon a huge banquet room. But there is something rather strange about the hall. Down the center is a long banquet table, but it is ten feet high—so high that no one in the hall can possibly reach the glorious food that is so generously piled upon it. However, with the aid of six-foot-long chopsticks provided each person, the food can be reached. But the chopsticks, being six feet long, prove impractical for conveying the food from table to mouth. It falls instead on the floor, where it is immediately gobbled up by swarms of dogs. The scene is one of frustration, hunger, and despair.

John has seen enough. Saint Peter leads him back to heaven. But heaven is the same huge banquet hall with the same ten-foot-high table piled up with delicious food. And all the saints are provided with the same six-foot-long chopsticks. The mood, however, is festive and joyous. Everyone has plenty to eat. The saints pick the food off the table, but instead of trying to eat it themselves, they feed one another. Thus no food is lost, and everyone eats very well. And such is the difference between heaven and hell.

Teaching stories are much better tools for conveying the experience of heaven and hell in all its ramifications and subtlety than are the techniques of philosophy and theology. We can identify with the stories and enter into them; we see in them a new way of experiencing the world. Having entered into this story, we can then return to our own world with the realization that wherever we are can be either heaven or hell. For heaven and hell do not depend upon where we are but rather upon how we live wherever we happen to be.

Initiation Stories

Religious stories often initiate us into new ways of being, seeing, and living in the world. They accomplish this purpose in the same way as teaching stories do. Ordinarily we believe that the world we take for granted is the real world. We believe that it is possible with a little effort to learn to function successfully in that world in a realistic and even profitable way. But the great religious traditions tell us that the ordinary way of living, commonsensical as it seems, is not the way to live to best advantage. Indeed, the way to true happiness as recommended by the great religious traditions seems to the average person foolish, perhaps even stupid or destructive. But if we can put this teaching into stories, if we can through story bring people to see the world in a way different from the usual—a way which within the framework of the story is obviously true—then the story might lure us into experimenting with the new point of view.

The Sufi tradition is very rich in just such teaching stories. Here's one I've modified slightly by using Western situations and people.

Once upon a time there was a very old and holy priest. One day the priest sat in his boat in the middle of the lake, fishing. As he sat, he heard drifting toward him over the waters a chant coming from a small hut on the shore. "Al-le-lu-IA, al-le-lu-IA, al-le-lu-IA."

As the priest listened, he thought to himself, "That chant is very ancient and holy; it has been claimed by holy tradition that such a chant has many miraculous powers. Indeed I have heard it said that if it is chanted correctly, one will be able to walk on water. To tell the truth, however, I myself have never been blessed with that power, nor have I known anyone who has. And unfortunately, this young man in the hut will never achieve that power, because he has learned the chant incorrectly. It is my duty as leader of the spiritual community to leave my fishing and go instruct this young man in the correct chant."

So the priest drew in his line, rowed to shore, and entered the hut where the young man was chanting.

"I have heard your chanting from out on the lake," said the priest, "and would like to commend your piety and devotion. But I have something to offer you from my own experience and learning. You are placing the emphasis upon the wrong syllable. Sacred tradition says that it should be sung, Al-le-LU-ia. I am sure that if you chant it this way you will make much spiritual progress."

The young man thanked the old priest very much. And as the old priest left the hut, he could hear the young man chanting, "Al-le-LU-ia, al-le-LU-ia." Pleased that he had done this good deed and put this young man squarely on the right path, the old priest climbed back into his boat and began rowing toward his fishing spot. He was barely halfway back when the sound of the chanting stopped. And when it began again, it had changed back to "Al-le-lu-IA, al-le-lu-IA."

The old priest frowned and mused sadly on the perversity of human nature. How hard it is, he thought, to break our old routines and embark upon the long and narrow road toward salvation. As he was thinking thus, he felt a tap on his shoulder. Startled, he turned around. There, standing on the water beside the boat in the middle of the lake, was the young man. "Father," he said, "I hate to bother you, but would you be so kind as to teach me the correct way of chanting the prayer again."

This story tells us more powerfully than any doctrine that the essence of spirituality lies, not in the way, or the words, or any other magic rites, but rather in what happens in the heart. The young man could chant his prayer in the wrong way, and yet if it came from his heart, he was able to walk on water.

These sacred stories are not merely means of entertainment. They are not stories to be heard once or twice and then discarded as we move on to something new. Our religious tradition supplies us with special stories we can take with us to nourish us throughout the rest of our lives' journeys. It will take the rest of our lives and all our experience to appreciate fully and exhaust these special tales. We need to enter these narratives more fully through meditation.

Entering into the Story

To meditate upon a story, choose a particular story and then enter into it as fully as possible. Imagine yourself present in the scene of the story. What did the people look like? What did they say to one another? Where have they come from? What has led them to be a part of this story? What are the different personalities like? What setting does the story take place in? Fill in all these details as vividly as possible.

Then go further. Enter into the story itself, assuming the major roles yourself. If it is a story about Jesus, begin by playing a person in the crowd. What would it be like to be a member of this group of people and witness what Jesus does? Then move from the crowd into each of the characters, including Jesus himself, experiencing the story anew from each of these personal viewpoints.

Finally, when you feel you have exhausted your possibilities for entering into the story, just sit with the story for a time in quiet. Perhaps the story has something more to say. Don't be too narrow in what you expect from the story. It may not provide you with any tremendous insight. It may simply grant you a feeling or an experience.

But we can go even further in our prayer with these sacred stories. The stories that are really important to us are the stories we manage to make our own. In the process of appropriating the stories, we change them in real and significant ways. Whether we are aware of the process or not, we have put our own special experience and insight into the stories.

We can witness this process through an experience of group prayer. Form a group to spend the evening sharing stories with one another. First the group must settle upon what kind of stories are to be shared. It must find a common story base. In this exercise, we'll concentrate upon stories shared by each member of the group; we're not interested here in sharing stories we haven't heard before. We want to see how the stories we tell are changed and assume our own coloration.

If, for instance, the group is composed of Christians or Jews, it might choose to explore stories from the religious tradition. If the group is a family, you may prefer stories about family members and events that have been cherished and retold at family gatherings. A more heterogeneous group may want to select Greek and Roman mythology, fairy-tales, or even plots from Shakespeare. The kinds of stories are not so important as the fact that each member of the group is familiar with the corpus of material and values certain stories within that material.

Next we sit in the group and tell our significant stories. And let's tell it as though none of the others had heard it before. Don't explain the story, but let the story explain itself. We want to tell people through the story itself just why that story is special to us. We want the others to appreciate and love that story just as we do. Take real poetic license with the story: we can exaggerate certain parts that we like or consider important. We may even want to change certain details to communicate more vividly.

Most of the time, however, we'll be listening rather than telling. And the listener's role is very important here. True, we have heard these stories many times. So this time, let's not listen for the main outlines—those we could recount in our sleep. Rather let's listen for what is original and new in this special telling. How has the person truly made the story her own or his own? Why is this story important to the teller? What does he or she find so appealing in this story?

After the stories are told, we might want to check out the originals in a few instances if there is any way to do so. Then we'll discover how each person has changed the story in some significant way. The narrator may even have changed it drastically so that it has indeed become a new and different story. Such a change should not be regarded as a fault. Rather, try to appreciate that the person has appropriated the story as his or her own and has brought to that story a unique experience and insight, enriching the story by the addition.

We might also continue the process by discussing just how the various stories have been appropriated by different members. Since each person has told a story we all already know, we may wish to share with each other various ways each of us has appropriated a particular story. As we share, exchange, and give stories in this way, we can come to a deeper appreciation of the very human gift of storytelling and story hearing.

Of course, we don't need a group in order to appropriate stories for ourselves. We do it all the time. Stories significant to us have been given to us as gifts. They belong to us, and there's no reason we can't enter into the story process and make these gifts even more fully our own. We can rewrite these stories, or better yet, in meditation the creative spirit within us might transform the stories so that they have even greater shaping power in our lives. You might want to try this with one of your favorite stories.

Many of Jesus' parables have no real ending. For example, the great parable of the prodigal son stops just before the final scene. The young man comes home; his father greets him, forgives him, and orders the banquet celebrating his return prepared. But then the elder son arrives from the fields very upset with what is happening. After all, he has remained home the whole time, working and helping his father. There has never been so great a feast put on for him.

The father acknowledges his older son's complaint. On the other hand, the younger son, the one they thought dead, has come home. That is great cause for rejoicing. There the parable ends.

But what happens? Does the elder brother ever go in to the banquet? We don't know. Jesus invites us to enter into the creation of the story by supplying our own ending. Such a tantalizing trick involves us in the story and makes the story a part of us.

We have also in our lives received traditional stories in a much more personal dress. In such stories, the events, persons, and the images may be from our personal lives, but the themes and plots belong to all of humanity. These personal traditional stories are called dreams, and we tell them to ourselves every night.

Dreams have formed an important part of most religious traditions. In the Judeo-Christian tradition, two of the great heroes—both named Joseph—have been dreamers. In the Old Testament, Joseph—a dreamer and interpreter of dreams—is hated by his brothers and sold into slavery in Egypt. But through his knowledge of dreams, he rises to a high position in the Egyptian court and eventually saves his father and brothers when they are driven to Egypt by a famine. All of this comes about because of his gift for dreams.

Joseph's namesake in the New Testament is the father of Jesus. He also receives messages from God through his dreams. Most of us believe that our dreams are very tenuous if not altogether meaningless or actually deceitful. Yet here is Joseph in a very difficult and compromising situation. The girl to whom he is betrothed is found to be pregnant by someone else. And the only help Joseph receives in resolving this dilemma comes in the shape of dreams. There he is told that Mary will give birth to the Messiah and that he should marry her. Joseph is exalted as a saint in Christianity today because he dared listen to his dreams and take them seriously as the voice of God. We need no better proof from our religious tradition of the validity of dreams as a gateway into the spiritual than these examples and many others in the Old and New Testaments.

But if we accept dreams as a valid route into the realm of the spirit, we are confronted with a dilemma: we either (1) believe that we do not dream, or (2) if we have received assurances that we must dream in order to even maintain our sanity, we then say we can never recall our dreams. Thus we too easily assume that work and prayer with dreams is not for us. But this situation can be changed; we can learn rather painlessly to remember our dreams. Indeed, dreaming is one of the simplest routes into the inner life.

In order to begin remembering our dreams, it is often enough to simply decide we will remember them. But in addition, we must value our dreams and take them seriously. Dreams are fragile creatures. If they see that they're not taken seriously and cherished, they're not likely to impose on us. But if we can convince our dreams that they're important to us, then they'll befriend us and make themselves remembered when we awaken.

To remember dreams, suggest to yourself before you go to sleep that you'll remember your dreams that night. Be as positive as possible. "I want to remember my dreams tonight" is not as good as "I will remember my dreams tonight." Say such a little phrase three or four times to yourself before going to sleep. In addition, keep a pad and pencil or small cassette recorder by your bedside so that as soon as you wake you can be reminded that you want to remember your dreams, and you'll have the materials immediately at hand to recover them.

Remembering Dreams

As you awaken from a dream, try not to do so too quickly. Don't jump out of bed, but remain for a few moments with your eyes shut. See if the dream comes back to you. If you can't recall it right away, pass through your mind some events and people in your life; the associations may trigger the dream. It is also very helpful to go back into the position from which you awoke. Often merely assuming the same sleep position floods the dream back into consciousness.

When you come to record your dreams either on cassette or eventually, in your journal, you want to record them in a special way—as though they were happening right now. Describe what happened in the present tense: not "I found myself in a dark place," but instead, "I find myself in a dark place." Keep the dream relatively pure; don't contaminate it with explanations or analysis. Tell the dream just as it occurred, without any additions. Of course if there were any explanations within the dream itself, you include those in your description of the dream. You also want to include within the dream your feeling states at various times in the dream, as well as how you felt as you awoke from the dream. All of this description should be entered in the dream-diary section of the journal.

Once you've recorded your dream, then, you can, if you wish, record any analysis of the dream in the life-diary of the journal. But more important, you want to record any associations you have to parts of the dream, as well as any ways in which you see the dream extending into your waking life. If the dream picked up on a recent incident in your life, record that incident. In the future you can always link your associations with the original dream by the dates in both sections of the journal.

Once you've begun to collect your dreams, you'll wish to begin working and praying with them. There are many techniques we can use to pray with our dreams without resorting to professional analysis. And our dream work begins not with any elaborate dream theory. Rather, just collect and appreciate your dreams as creations from your inner self. They have something to tell us. If we give them sufficient time and attention, they'll reveal what they have to say in their own special personal language. If we spend enough time with our dreams, we'll come to learn the images and languages they use. Many of these images and symbols will be peculiar to ourselves alone; and we can't read about them in textbooks on dreaming. But we can learn to read them, just as we learned to speak our native tongue. With time, they become clear.

Dream Interviews

You can also interview your dreams. Here again it is important that you assume nothing. Take, for example, a dream in which a tree appears. The question you want to ask is not necessarily what the tree means. Instead, try to keep to the question, "What is a tree?" Perhaps this is a particular kind of tree with yellow flowers. Then you ask, "What is a yellow-flowered tree?" Supply all the associations you can to that object. What is a tree to you? You might assume everybody knows what a tree is and that the response is the same for everyone. But especially when we're dealing with dream figures, we're often confronted by very personal and important symbols.

To me, a tree may have associations of fear and hurt because I once fell out of one and broke a leg. For another person, the tree may be the primary image of beauty because it has always been the favorite creation of nature. It is important that we discover for ourselves just what these dream images can represent. What is a tree, what is a gate, what is a cloud? As objects appear in our dreams, let's question ourselves on what they are for us. And let's take no object for granted by assuming we know just exactly what it means. Although we'll employ techniques used and developed by Freud, Jung, and others, let's leave their overall theories aside here at the beginning of our work with dreams.

Role Playing with Dreams

At some point, you may want to enter into the different parts and roles that appear in your dream. After all, you are the creator of your dream; at a deep level of your being, you have created the dream and decided just how it should move. So in some sense you are part of your dream. To discover what the dream is saying, you'll sometimes find it a help to enter into the dream just as you entered into the stories, assuming the different roles that appear in the dream.

Let us say that your mother formed a part of a dream, but you're not quite sure what she was doing there. You might shed light on her appearance by going into meditation and then reviewing the dream from her perspective in it. You can also ask her why she is there, where she has come from, how she feels about this dream. If you enter into your dreams this way, they often open up for you and share their secrets. And don't restrict yourself to playing people in your dream interviews. If the dream has significant objects, they are a part of you as well. So if a mysterious tree appears in a dream, it might behoove you to reenter the dream from the vantage point of the tree.

We might also expand our dreams just as we expanded the stories. Reenter the dream in meditation, and reenact it. But as you do so, you needn't restrict yourself to the original dream. Allow the dream to expand and develop. You may remember only an incomplete scene. But that small scene is still a key to your inner life. In meditation, that seed could crystallize a whole realm of experience.

Expanding Dreams

Choose a dream that you'd like to explore further. Go into a quiet meditative state, and recall the dream to mind. Be with the dream, and allow it to expand. See where the dream wants to take you. What further story does it wish to tell? Realize that this is a prayer experience, and remind yourself that you're here to get in touch with yourself.

Don't be overly manipulative. Instead, try to achieve a delicate balance between your own conscious manipulation of the dream (which forms part of the work because you're in a state of consciousness) and the hints, suggestions, and traces you receive from your unconscious self, supplying you with clues about how the dream truly wishes to work itself out. The work of dream expansion—if it is carried on correctly and carefully, with some delicacy—is not mere game playing. It can really open you to your deeper self while you're awake. This work should of course be recorded in the prayer-experiences section of your journal.

As you continue to collect your dreams, you'll notice that certain images, themes, places, and incidents occur again and again. You might want to work on a dream collage consisting of three or four dreams that share something in common.

Dream Collage

Collect the dreams you wish to work on in the collage. Then read them over and go into a quiet state of meditation. In the meditation, allow the different dreams to interact with one another. Let them play with one another and form different clusters. Allow various elements from one dream to enter into the others, or take some elements from each dream and give them the opportunity to create a new dream. By giving these dreams the opportunity to come into contact with one another whole new insights are often given to you.

These are just some of the many ways that you can begin to pray with your dreams. Of course whenever you work on your dreams, you'll want to describe the experiences in the prayer-experience section of your journal. Begin by telling just what your experiment is. Record the experience as fully as you can. Naturally you'll want to record the experience while it is actually going on. With a little practice, you can learn to write in the journal without disturbing your meditation. Or, if this is too difficult, record the experience very soon after the prayer is over.

Perhaps you wish to explore a certain figure who recurs in various dreams, or a certain mood you're left with as a result of different dreams, or the fact that a cluster of dreams all occurred the same night, or finally you might want to work with certain dreams that just seem to belong together.

Life Stories

The primary story in our lives is not given to us by our tradition, whether public or private; it is the story our day-to-day existence is creating. Our lives, no matter how pedestrian they may seem to us, are telling a story. It certainly has a definite beginning, and (although we may not like to think of it) an ending as well. But the story in between is our own unique narrative. People from the time of Augustine (who in the West invented this genre) have been fascinated with the experience of writing their autobiographies. Although we might not consider the autobiography today a prayer form, it did begin as a prayer. And it fits our definition of prayer: as the process that expands our awareness. Augustine's *Confessions* are indeed prayer; he told his life to his Creator.

Autobiography is the recollection, from a certain point of time, of our life's unfoldment. The construction of autobiographies can be a way of praying. Each of us should be able to construct a series of autobiographies: there are many ways of telling the story of our life. Writing an autobiography sounds overwhelming because it implies that we need to record everything in our lives—all actions, thoughts, desires, beliefs, loves, hatreds, friendships, dialogues, and so on. Such a task is obviously impossible unless we spend the entire remainder of our lives engaged in it. But each autobiography is told, whether or not the author realizes it, from a very selective and limited point of view. Consider Augustine's religious confessions, Frank Harris's *My Life and Loves,* and Dante's *Divine Comedy* as just three diverse examples. So as we enter this process of life recollection, we not only tell the life from a different point of time but we also bring to each attempt the concerns and interests of this present moment in our lives. The prayer experience acknowledges this natural process and actually cultivates it to our own benefit.

If you construct your autobiographies along certain definite and articulated points of view, you'll be exploring a number of different lenses through which you may examine your life. You might choose to explore your intellectual journey. What ideas have motivated you? What has been the history of your education in both the narrow sense of your schooling and in the broader sense of your "being led forth" into life? Or consider your life on the emotional level. What have been the friendships, rivalries, and loves that have nourished you?

From the spiritual point of view, what has been the evolution of your inner life? During what times has the inner life been very important? And conversely when did the inner life seem rather remote or perhaps even nonexistent? This inner life would include conversion experiences, times when we have felt arid and dry, times when we have been flooded with a sense of fulfillment, and times when we have felt whole and at peace with the world.

What has been the history of your life in your vocation? Such an autobiography would include the various tasks you have felt called to, a history of your work, and an overview of your creations. It would also include the history of your relationship to your work and the meanings different jobs have had for you. You certainly don't think of your childhood chores, the job that put you through school, and your present profession in the same way, nor did they affect your life in the same way. But they all are a part of your life and had a part in bringing you to this present moment.

Finally, you might want to focus upon one very specific period of your life. You could then explore that limited time in some depth. You might then relate that special period to others that went before it (what were the seeds that germinated there?) as well as to those that followed. What were the seeds created during this special time that came to flower later? These are some of the different ways we can structure the autobiographies that we work on in the prayer-experience section of our journals.

Once you have chosen a point of view, you next draw up an outline of your life according to this particular vantage point. Say that you wish to construct your autobiography along the lines of your spiritual development. What have been the turning points, the passages, the crises that you've traversed? You should be able in each of these autobiographies to chart from ten to fifteen turning points in your life—events, meetings, feelings that have proven significant. When you have jotted down this outline, you can go back and fill in the different sections, exploring each turning point in more detail.

Autobiographical Turning Points

A few months ago, I began work on an autobiography from the viewpoint of my own spiritual growth. As I created an outline, I found most of the turning points hinged upon quite external events, such as my conversion or my ordination to the priesthood. I used these rather external events as pegs upon which I could weave my fuller recollections of my inner life.

And as I related and recovered the inner processes and experiences that went along with these external events, I discovered my inner life opening into my awareness in a way that it hadn't done before. Previously I'd thought that outside of a few dramatic changes, my inner life was pretty stable and even dull. But in the process of recollecting,

I came in touch with many forgotten experiences. And indeed my spiritual life now was very inadequately described by my initial outline.

True, events such as conversion and ordination were great spiritual turning points in my life, but I often found that the inner turning point did not actually coincide with the event. So I went back to construct a much fuller and richer history of my inner development. This new outline was a much closer reflection of my development than the first. By going through this process, I know myself better now. In prayer, the experience of the moment is paramount. We are not concerned so much with the goal as with the process of entering into our histories to reclaim them for our present.

Your life is an archeological treasure trove. Your entire past is not dead and buried; it waits to be utilized in new and different ways. Here is the rich soil from which your life can receive nutriment and grow. If you keep the soil loose, your life today can be alive and rich. In the writing and praying of autobiography, your life stays in motion, ever developing, ever renewing.

Creating Stories

Creating stories from the fertility of our imaginations can also provide prayer experiences. All of us have at some time or another joined in the creation of stories, if only to exaggerate a true event in the interests of gossip or to create a joke. It provides great pleasure and brings us fully alive. So in our prayer life, let's set aside some time for the creation of stories.

You may consider yourself too unimaginative to write good stories. But in prayer, we create stories just as we create autobiographies—not for the booksellers but rather for ourselves.

If you think you need help in stimulating your imagination, you might use the Tarot cards mentioned in a previous chapter (page 84). These cards depict elemental powerful images shared by all humanity. They crop up in our myths, our folktales, and our dreams. These images come forth from deep within us and reveal the contents and workings of our inner world.

Begin your meditation by selecting one card from the deck. Treat this card as though it is one moment of a continuing story. In your meditation, explore the characters and objects on the card. How did they get there? What is happening now on the card? What will happen in the moments that will unfold after this present moment shown on the card?

You can also use the Tarot in a more complex fashion. Once again, start with the premise that each card shows one scene from the continuing story. But now you pick five or six cards at random or by selecting those that interest you. When you have selected your cards, lay them in front of you. Then you can arrange them in various combinations. While you're in a prayerful state, allow the cards to arrange themselves to tell a story, much as a cartoon strip highlights a story in a few sketches.

Don't become so anxious about this process that you manipulate and force the cards into a story. Give the cards and your inner self the time and the space they need. If a story is there, it will come to the surface, provided you wait in silence.

Working with our inner selves is a lot like fishing. Impatience gets us nowhere and often only succeeds in scaring away the fish. While we fish, we have the opportunity to wait in silence and do nothing. We have that same opportunity whenever we pray. We don't create the stories out of nothing. They come from deep within us. And if they come from that secret place, they have the possibility of revealing to us the core of our own beings.

The good storyteller doesn't tell stories just to teach. Rather he also is like a fisherman. His stories are beautiful lures by which he hopes to tempt us into entering into a different world (a better one, let's hope, than the poor fish goes to when it bites the hook). The storyteller wants to entertain, to fascinate, to excite, to tantalize. And we should look for these same elements in our own stories. We shouldn't primarily be concerned about what they mean. Indeed often the best stories will seem quite resistant to any meaning we try to attach to them. But they do not speak through our intellects; they have a more secret door into our beings.

Poetry

At the very peak of the story-prayer experience, we enter into the sacred realm of poetry. Here individual words cease to be important. For the poetry is really the music we hear behind the words. As we explore our own prayer deeper and deeper through stories, dreams, recollections, and imagination, we'll often receive gift poems. In our meditations, we'll find phrases or even whole poems coming to us.

And we'll discover that the words themselves only serve a shimmering melody, which sings behind them.

As we go through our prayer experiences, let's collect these gifts—these magic phrases and poems. We can enjoy them, cherish them, and use them as keys into our own inner life. We should enter them in the prayer-gift section of the journal.

Behind the words of our stories, the images of our dreams, the events of our autobiographies, the actions of our stories—behind all of these is a music whose sound is silence, a flame whose light is darkness, a love whose power is weakness, and a person whom many call God.

Fifteen

The Prayer of Persons

As work on the body leads into the prayer experience of sport, so work on the spirit prepares us for the prayer experience of persons— by far our peak possible experience of prayer. The best and fullest experience of prayer is the encounter with another person, whether that person be another human being or God. And actually prayer with persons is always prayer with God. Even if the external object is another human, in prayer we are communicating with the depths of that other person.

When we enter the depths of another, we enter into the presence of God. On the basis of this insight, Catholicism makes marriage a sacrament. In the act of loving another, we discover and experience the love that is God. The primary experience of this prayer between persons is love, and Christian tradition says that God's primary characteristic is love. Nor does this mean only that God is loving; Christianity dares to go further and say that God is love itself.

Mirror Meditation

The first prayer experience possible with another comes back to our adventure in becoming aware of our own spirit. When we look at another person, we are actually examining a mirror image of ourselves. And when we deal with another, we're in some sense dealing with ourselves. In the myth of Adam and Eve, Eve is created for Adam's fulfillment: he is not complete without her; hence his loneliness. (And lest I sound chauvinistic, we could as easily say that Eve needs Adam for her fulfillment, hence her loneliness.) God himself, in Christian experience, is not alone. Rather he is three persons who share the same Godhead. Community and society lie at the very basis of human existence and fulfillment. To be a total hermit is to be inhuman.

The other person is a reflection of who I am. And when I learn who you are, I learn how we're alike. And at the same time, I learn how you (and therefore I) are unique. Often I'm surprised to learn that things I consider most unusual about myself, indeed the ways in which I consider myself strange and freaky, are the ways in which we turn out to be alike. And conversely, the qualities I consider common sometimes are revealed as unique to me.

To take an example from prayer. A man in a course I was teaching told me he was tremendously relieved when I said that the most common problem in prayer is distraction. He had never heard this said before and had always regarded himself as working under a great handicap when he meditated. Now you might think this man was pretty blind to an obviously common human experience. But the blindness of others is so much easier to spot than our own. And blindness cannot be considered relative. If I'm blind in any area, the important thing is not why I am blind but rather that I can't see. We are all blind to our uniqueness and our commonness. And if we don't come to see ourselves in the reflection of others, our blindness can never be cured. We must risk exploring our mutual blindnesses if we are ever to come into the light.

If there is another person willing to do this exercise with you, it can help penetrate your blindness. First each person sits in front of his or her own small face mirror, placed about two feet in front of the face. For twenty minutes, meditate upon the image of your own face. Do not analyze, judge, or criticize. Let the image simply be in front of you.

With this first exercise completed, continue the meditation on the face of your partner. Sit facing one another with knees touching. This will bring the other person's face about the same distance away as your mirror image. For the next twenty minutes, meditate upon your friend's face in the same way you did upon your own. Simply be aware of the experience. Don't seek for anything. Don't ask yourself questions. Don't judge or criticize. Be aware of the other person looking at you and of yourself looking at the other. Sometimes this meditation provides an incredible experience of communication beyond the level of words, thoughts, or gestures. Laughter sometimes occurs in this meditation. Let the laughter come. It is a sign of uneasiness. If it is allowed to happen, it will help you relax and feel at ease with the meditation. And it will soon depart, leaving you with your meditation.

Prayer with other people calls us toward totality and wholeness. As we progress through our lives, we have a constant temptation to isolate one part of our being, whether it be body, mind, or spirit. We think of and value ourselves for that favorite part rather than for our whole person. But such thought is very limiting not only to friends and lovers but also to ourselves.

Let me share with you an experience I had with a very close friend. This particular friend might as well be my identical twin: we think and feel alike, we share many of the same views of life, and we have had frequent experiences of thinking about the same thing at the same time. A few months ago, I went back East and had the opportunity to see him again. In the excitement of reunion, we had much to share. I felt a real need to talk, but I also felt an effort and strain to keep the conversation flowing: I was running out of things to say. Finally Frank said to me, "Why don't you shut up?" (He, like myself, has not been corrupted by the art of subtlety.) I suddenly realized we didn't have to fill the air with talk. We could just be together, and that was enough.

I had been working under the assumption that I had to deal with Frank totally on the mind level. But our friendship wasn't confined to the mental level, although that is the part of me that I mistakenly value. Our friendship involved a recognition and love of kindred spirits; on the level of spirit, words are not necessary. It is enough just to be together. When Frank told me to shut up, instead of feeling hurt or angry, I felt an immense relief: "Thank God I can stop this chatter because even I am running out of things to say."

It also drives me crazy that people today feel a necessity to talk during a film. Why can't people enjoy a film together in silence? Why must they incessantly share their shallow likes and dislikes with one another? Are we so totally restricted to words and actions for communication that heart cannot speak to heart in silence? Talking and noise are fine at a popular film like *Star Wars* that asks us to cheer the heroes and heroines and boo the villains. But at a film where the artist is making a serious statement about life, this stupid chatter is aggravating. During the event, why not give ourselves over to the spirit? We can discuss the experience later. Art and films are meant to be enjoyed with others. It makes a difference whether I see a film alone or with someone else, even though never a word is spoken throughout. It is enough to be together as a great artist shares with us his or her world of the spirit.

Body and Sexuality

We have a great propensity to limit our bodies. We're overly preoccupied with sexuality, and we fail to consider that our bodies can be employed in nongenital ways. We forbid men to have any physical contact with one another outside the "good clean fun" of punching, kicking, or tripping one another in contact sports such as boxing or football. We have branded practically all other forms of touching sexual. So men are not allowed to embrace or do anything beyond a firm quick handshake. When we follow this kind of philosophy, we limit our bodies severely. After all, the body is the primary instrument of communication. These limiting customs are breaking down today, but many people are still stuck in them.

A few years ago, a film appeared that, although it was popular because it was sensational, also generated much adverse criticism because of its purported lack of taste. The film was *The Devils* by Ken Russell. One of the most shocking scenes concerned a nun who had sexual fantasies with the body of Christ on a crucifix. Many people considered such an idea abhorrent and blasphemous. But as Ken Russell, himself a convert to Catholicism, pointed out, such fantasies not only do occur with frequency in the religious imagination but also they are not really bizarre, abhorrent, or even abnormal. The fault lies with a culture that refuses to allow sexuality any relation to spirituality. That culture wants a group of disembodied angels offering pure unsullied worship of the holy of holies. But in Catholicism, the sacrament of marriage—which is consummated only by the sexual act—is a vehicle for experiencing God in his fullness. And in Christianity, the central doctrine (as celebrated in the great hymn of Ambrose) is that God did not shrink from a woman's womb but took on himself our full humanity. Jesus breathed, cried, laughed, excreted, and had wet dreams just like the rest of us. How can we leave the body out of spirituality when God thought it so important to take on a human body completely and live out a full life in it?

The element of sexuality in our friendships makes us uptight. Or today we consider ourselves liberated if we bring any element of sexuality in a relationship right out into the open, hopping into bed with anyone who arouses any interest at all.

We are bodily persons, and we will have bodily feelings for the important people in our life. Why should that make us uptight? On the other hand, why should we treat a friend in the same way of full sexuality that we reserve for that person who is unique and special to us? There is nothing wrong with sexual feelings. Yet they need not always be fully expressed: if we bring all our relationships to the same level, we will find that all our relationships are common and none of them reach very deeply.

Sexuality has both a bodily and a spiritual dimension. In the context of intimacy, trust, and commitment, a relationship can open into a spiritual dimension precisely through sexual union. And in other friendships, there will also be an element of sexuality. That is normal and good. But not every relationship should or can achieve the level of intimacy where that sexuality can be fully shared. In some ways, a sexual intimacy makes impossible some of the beauties of friendship. The friend is different from the lover. The friend can experience things the lover cannot. But sometimes we make the mistake of thinking the lover is merely the friend who has moved into a greater degree of intimacy through sexuality.

We reject the bodily side of our spiritual life. Our western traditions have not been much concerned with the body. There is no Christian or Jewish equivalent to Hatha Yoga. And as I mentioned earlier, it is very strange for us to consider sports a form of spirituality. Catholicism did maintain a minimum of body prayer in things such as genuflection, kneeling, standing, the thumbing of rosary beads, moving from station to station of the cross, and the idea of pilgrimage. But much of even that mere taste of body prayer has been lost since the Second Vatican Council. Not only must body prayer be regained in new ways; it must be allowed to flower.

Massage

For the sake of convenience, let's group three types of prayer with people—types of prayer that involve our three divisions of body, mind, and spirit. Prayer with the body is involved with the sense of touch, understood in its broadest sense. The love that body prayer celebrates is the love of eros or sexuality understood in its widest (more than genital) sense.

Massage is one possible body prayer with persons. In the experience of massage, we have opportunity to give another person pleasure and relaxation, and we have the opportunity to receive the gift of massage from another. The learning experience here is twofold: learning to give pleasure, and—perhaps even more important for us—learning how to accept the gift of pleasure from another.

I have a very good friend, who enjoys massage. She wanted to massage my head. I went through agonies of guilt about receiving this gift and giving nothing in return. She is doing this nice thing for me, and I have nothing to give in return. I do not know how to massage, and massage is an art, not just a rubdown. I could only finally allow her to massage me when I realized that perhaps she received as much pleasure out of giving the massage as I did out of receiving it.

The most obvious body prayer is of course sexuality itself. And through this most intimate sharing, two people can come to experience one another and almost merge into a new unity.

Mental prayer with persons uses conversation as its technique. The love expressed in this prayer is friendship, which C. S. Lewis once described as the love of shared interests. At first I thought this a rather limited definition of friendship, because friendship can and does go far beyond the limits of interests and ideas. But at least in this prayer, I am talking about friendship that springs out of shared interests.

Conversation and Listening

In true conversation, we learn to listen to one another and share with one another our interests and the ways in which we see the world. In friendship, we can learn to experience the world through another human being's eyes and senses. What does that other person love? How does she or he respond to the world?

Friendship can not only tell us of the things we share with others but can also expand our own world through new interests and experiences. One of my particular passions is opera, and I have felt like a real freak because I know intimately few other people who share this passion. (I have somehow never tried to establish my friendships on the basis of opera.) And I have kept my interest in opera very much to myself as a private passion, as though it were my personal pornography collection that I'm ashamed of, although I love this art. I have kept it concealed because I just didn't believe other people could really enjoy it. And I'd become defensive when someone would question me about opera, asking me to share my love with them. I would immediately suspect their motives; after all why should they want to love this impossible art form? And deep inside I believed my devotion to opera was weird, although it is one of the forces that have influenced deeply my way to seeing the world.

But now I'm learning that my friends can ask me about opera with genuineness, not because they want to become opera freaks, but simply because they want to gain a better understanding of what has shaped my own vision of the world. They want to know what I value in opera; why do I spend my time with it? And if they can discover that, perhaps they can come to know me better.

I see this same process of friendship emerging in myself as well. I want to know about my friends' interests and passions that I don't share. And my intentions aren't necessarily to become passionate about the same things but rather to enlarge my own experience through my friends and to come to know my friends better. There is no need to live our lives only through our own passions and experiences; that would be very limiting. We can live, love, and enjoy whole universes of experience through the lives of our friends. My friend Frank, whom I mentioned a few pages ago, is a horticulturist. Through our friendship, I now know there is more to a plant than just the fact that it makes the environment green. Another friend introduced me to the mysteries of rock music. Here was a musical world I knew nothing about. Today I'm not a wild enthusiast of rock—I still do not prefer it to opera. But I do enjoy rock, and I owe this part of my life entirely to Gene. I came to know, appreciate, and enjoy rock through his eyes and experience. And I found that rock could speak to me and I could enjoy it in my own right.

Finally, spiritual prayer with another person involves the love of agape, the love that is charity, the love of the other for her or his own sake. The technique of this prayer form is dialogue. This prayer involves the creation of intimacy between persons. Unlike the prayer of friendship, we're not talking here about interests and ideas; rather our content centers on what is most ourselves—our private thoughts, experiences, and feelings. This prayer is summed up in the motto of Cardinal John Henry Newman: heart speaks to heart. This is a prayer without masks, and—in its full flowering—without censorship. This kind of prayer happens primarily in marriage and in friendships that have moved beyond the stage of shared interest. It is this experience of intimacy that—once it has been established—may be celebrated on the bodily level through sexual union. It is not common, and when it occurs, it is cherished as a moment that makes life worth living.

The dialogue of true intimacy is rare—it does not often come our way. It may happen only once or twice in a lifetime if at all. And when it does occur, although it is a result of much hard work and

135

perhaps pain, it is experienced, not as something earned, but rather as a glorious gift. But the prayer of intimate exchange can be learned now. Although its fullest experience and expression occur in actual exchange with another living and present person, yet it is possible to initiate dialogue with people now even if we or that other person are not yet ready for or capable of actual intimacy.

We carry all of our significant others—the people with whom intimacy is possible or desirable—within us. Because of various obstacles and blockages, we might never be able to dialogue with people who have tremendous influence over our lives today. Perhaps they are not ready to dialogue, or the actual relationship is stuck in a rut, or the person is no longer present, or that person perhaps doesn't even know how important he or she is to us (such a person may be a teacher we knew only as a member of a class). All of these people are still available for dialogue in our prayer. We can enter into deep and even revelatory dialogue with them, achieving breakthroughs in our interior relations to them that may never be possible in actual life.

Perhaps your relationship to your mother is still limiting your own life. Maybe there is no real opportunity to deal with her in actuality because both of you will end up in your own defenses, which will prevent any growth in the relationship. But in your private dialogue you can open yourself to her, and perhaps in this dialogue, you can actually move beyond your present blockages and enter into a new relationship, at least on your part, a move that will free you from the old constricted ways of being that your present relationship imposes.

Dialogue

We conduct this dialogue by first calming and quieting ourselves and entering into a receptive and prayerful state. Then we spend some time making that person we wish to dialogue with present to us. Let's imagine their physical presence, their way of speaking, and what they bring with them from their own experience: what does the story of their life look like?

When you feel that the person you wish to talk with is in some sense present to you, then you can begin to write the dialogue in the prayer-experience section of the journal. Begin the dialogue on the surface. Don't start with the deep and profound questions. That isn't the way you'd start an actual living dialogue. First you'd become comfortable with one another, each asking how the other is and is feeling. Then let the dialogue take its natural course. After a while, you'll feel the dialogue moving under its own power. No longer will you feel you are putting words in the other person's mouth; you'll actually feel the presence of that other person in the dialogue and will experience the mystery of the other there.

As we come to know the spirit within others, we discover that it is the same spirit that gives life to our own being: what Christians call the Holy Spirit. Dialogue is the consummate Christian prayer technique because it is an experience of the way in which God operates: the persons of the Trinity commune with one another in the awe-filled intimate dialogue of love, which is the Godhead.

The final goal of our prayer experience is the experience of the divine. Actually our human desire has always been to become divine. All the prayer forms we have discussed aim toward that same goal. And the great spiritual traditions also affirm that the power at the center of the universe, which we usually name God, strives with all its might to achieve the same goal. God wants us to share his divinity just as much as we want to share it.

Sixteen

Epilogue

I feel as though I have sneakily led you up to the church doors in the last couple of chapters. Even the name of my sponsor has been spoken. I hope you won't consider it a dirty trick on my part; it's just my natural self showing through. And as long as we are at the door, why don't you come inside for a moment or two? Throughout this book, you've seen me in a number of different moments—the preoccupied fool standing in an airport lobby with a flower in his lapel and a Hare Krishna magazine in his hand, wondering how he got ripped off; the scared teen-ager who shivered through every gym class for fear he would have to show his lack of abilities in sports; the kid who took out his anger on ivory piano keys and was transformed into the glory of music; the friend whose friend tells him to shut up and who takes no offense because that friend is speaking the truth. Well, if you have seen that much, you might as well see all of me: the public me, the preacher.

Come on inside. The building is big, cold, and perhaps oppressive. It looks more like a museum of modern art than a church. But there is warmth inside because of the people. And they are all ordinary people like yourself, who come together here for an hour a week to be a little more open and friendly to one another. I'm sure they would welcome you and ask you to sit with them. You might want to sit with my friends Brian and Mary (she's the one who gave me my first massage and bore with me throughout the writing of this book). Dan and Dianne are there; they're the only couple who look like quintessential Berkeley people, and they are actually from New York. Nancy (who typed the book for me) is there leading the music with a smile no one can resist. There are a lot of college students, freshly back from Christmas vacation.

It is the Sunday after New Year's—the feast of Epiphany, when the three kings came bearing gifts to the Christ child. Yours truly, like many others there is recovering from a cold. I'm tired and exhausted but happy because last night the last chapter of this book was completed. I didn't get to sleep till 4 A.M., but I'm here. Come on in and join us.

Here at the beginning of Jesus' life, three weird characters—astrologers and kings—show up on the doorstep with gifts prophetic of who this child is and who he is destined to become. I'd like to pull all of us into this beautiful story, because I believe there have been kings in our own lives who, like these three kings, have come to us bearing gifts that reveal to us who we are and who we are destined to become. I can think of three such kings in my own life, and as I speak of them, I invite you to cast your thoughts back over your own lives and remember the kings who have appeared on your doorstep.

My first king goes by the name of Frank, and when you first see him, you would never think of him as a king, but perhaps rather as the court jester. Frank brings me the gift of gold—a gift for kings. And I like to think Frank's gift is a golden mirror, because I have seen myself in him. For Frank is my twin, my double, although no relation by blood. But after knowing him for a short time, I saw how our interests, feelings, thoughts, and makeup were similar if not identical. In fact, mutual friends who enjoy us both separately often feel we are just too much for them together.

Frank's golden mirror has helped me because—like most of us—I don't like myself all that much. I see so much that I would like different about me. I don't want to stick out in a crowd; I want to be part of the group. Yet I'm different. And sometimes when I catch my reflection off guard in a mirror, the word that rises to my lips is *Schmo*. We don't like our freakiness—we want to be divine, or at the very least different.

But as I grew to know Frank and saw more and more of myself reflected in him, and as I grew to love him, I suddenly realized that if he could have all my awful peculiarities of thought and behavior and yet be lovable, perhaps those same qualities could be lovable in myself. I quickly discovered that Frank was not really a court jester, but a king in disguise. And here he was a king bringing me a golden mirror—a gift fit for a king.

I'm sure all of us have been visited by kings bearing gifts of gold for us that tell us we are OK—that we too are of royal blood. People have surprised us because we saw so much of ourselves in them and were

139

yet able to love them. They have been our parents, our brothers and sisters, our lovers, friends, husbands, and wives. And we have treasured them and considered ourselves fortunate to know them. And through them, we have seen that we too are kings—we, even *Schmos* that we are, are all right.

The child whose glory we celebrate today is also a king, and he also brings us a gift of gold. When we see him here today—a baby in his mother's arms—when we realize that he is destined to live a life just like ours—through the joys and pains of childhood, the glandular eruptions of puberty, the heartbreak of first love, the ecstasy of friendships, the doubts about vocation, the betrayal of trust, and the fears and nightmares of death—perhaps we can then see that it isn't so bad to be a human being. God didn't shrink away from living our life—humanity must be of royal blood—it was no disgrace in God's eyes to become one of us.

The second king comes from the Far East with an exotic name and title—Tarthang Tulku Rimpoche. He is a reincarnate Tibetan lama (how noble can you get?) and he lives in Berkeley, where he has brought the sacred teachings of his religion to share with Americans. I have known and admired him for over a year. And at times my fantasy has been to remove my shoes, kneel before him, and ask that he take me as his disciple. For he is where I would like to be.

I have not acted out my fantasy, but I know what his response would be. "Rimpoche," I would say, in my humble kneeling posture, "take me as your disciple and teach me all you know."

Rimpoche would smile, and in his broken English, he would say no.

Indeed he has already done this in a different way. A few weeks ago, I went to a seminar Rimpoche conducted on Buddhism and Christianity. Shortly after we began, Rimpoche asked if there were any Christian priests present. I raised my hand, and he looked at me with what seemed great respect—why, I don't know. Later in the seminar, he turned to me out of the blue and asked, "You are a priest. Now you talk. Tell me about faith. What is it?"

I was struck dumb. "I don't know what to say," I blurted out. "I've come to learn from you. I don't think I have anything to give you. I'm just here to learn."

From the twinkle in his eyes, I could see uncomfortably that Rimpoche did not accept my protest. In his eyes, I was a priest—and he wanted to hear from me as a priest. In his hands, I saw the gift of frankincense—the incense used in priestly rituals the world over. It is a gift only priests would give one another, and here was Rimpoche giving it to me. He was saying, "No. You are not my disciple. We are brothers. We are both priests, and we walk the same road, each in his own traditions. And as we walk together, we can help one another as brothers."

In the East, there is much giving of gifts. But the teacher never gives the disciple a gift. It is always the other way around. The teacher only gives gifts to his friends and comrades. And Rimpoche gave me the gift of saying I was valuable to him, and he needs me to help him walk his own path. In his eyes, I learned to revalue my own priesthood, my own ministry.

When the child Jesus grows up, he will bring us all a similar gift of frankincense. Christians have always called Jesus the Son of God, or God himself. And what does Jesus call us in return? His brothers and sisters. And he says that his Father is our Father as well.

In the life of each of us, someone has played the part of this second king and told us that we're valuable, we're holy, and we're rooted in goodness. We belong, and therefore we are holy; we stand together, and therefore we are rooted; we are signs of God's presence in the world, and therefore we are priests each in her or his own right.

The third king is tragic. He bears the gift of myrrh, the perfume used to anoint the dead. This gift of myrrh looks forward to Jesus' own death, even here in the joy of his birth. And this third sad king has appeared in our lives as well. For me he was a silent king; he never spoke a human word or even understood one. He was a king who lived little less than a year, and yet within that brief time he gave more to me and others than many kings give throughout a long reign. This king, like the king worshipped by the three astrologers, was a mere infant. His name was Matthew.

Being a priest, I have to live family life vicariously. And over the last few years, I have been adopted into the family of Faith and Mark. We had known one another and been best friends for three years before Matthew was born. So in a sense, Matthew was my spiritual child. He was born a couple of months premature, and he was one of a set of twin boys. His brother was born dead. Soon after birth, Matthew developed meningitis. Things came to a climax six months later when the doctors told Faith and Mark the tragic news that Matthew had no brain at all.

All they could do was take him home and care for him until he died. Three months later, he did die, and some people might lament that his life was useless. The only comfort was that he never suffered. I can only speak for myself, but Matthew's life was not useless. Indeed, like the child we celebrate today, he was the greatest of my kings.

141

Matthew's life could not be defended or explained or rationalized. It was tragic. And yet it was not without meaning for those of us who knew him because Matthew taught me something about living, about what it means to be alive. This child had no brain, no thoughts, no dreams, no future—and yet he drew breath and he lived. He lived his nine months, which is all he had, and in that nine months, he was alive to those of us who knew him.

I have lived much of my life by not living. I have been waiting to live, hoping that if my dreams came true, then I could really live; wishing that I were someone else, and then I could really live, wanting to follow exotic Eastern priests and kings who could somehow teach me how to live. But here was king Matthew, who had no time to wait because his living at all was a miracle, who didn't hope his dreams came true because he was incapable of dreaming, who could never become anyone else but who he was, and who could not be taught by anyone because he was unteachable. And yet Matthew drew breath and lived a miraculous nine months. When he died, we all felt a presence gone from our lives, because he had really lived. Without dreams or hopes or plans for the future, he had drawn breath and lived. He gave me myrrh—the gift of my own death. And with his gift—the gift of his own life—I have put down some of the hopes and dreams that keep me from living here and now. A little more today than before, I draw breath and live. And I say, "This is enough. This is sufficient. This is what it means to be alive."

Matthew's gift of myrrh—the gift of death—helped me to wake up to life. I hope that in your life, there has been someone who by living in all simplicity near the threshold of death has taught you how to live yourself. This child the three kings worship today will grow up and through his own untimely dying will teach millions of people what it means to be alive.

Being Christians, we must finally come to the realization that there is really only one king who stands behind and illumines all the many kings in our lives. Behind Frank, who brings the gift of gold that tells me I am a king, I see the glory of the Messiah. Behind Tarthang Tulku Rimpoche, who brings his brother priest the sweet fragrance of frankincense, I behold the flesh-and-blood humor and humanity of the Christ. And behind Matthew, who taught me how to live, I see the one anointed by God for death, who, having faced that death in obedience because he could do nothing else, now lives forever.

Three kings appear at the birth of Jesus with gifts that foretell who he is and who he will become. Kings have appeared in our lives as well with these same gifts. As Jesus grew in the strength and wisdom of

God, he indeed showed forth who he was and became who he was destined to be. Have we become who the kings say we are—a royal people, priests of God's presence in the world, and destined to live simply forever? We can, you know.

Feast of the Epiphany, 1978
Berkeley, California

Bibliography

This is a where-do-we-go-from-here bibliography. Obviously the fields of spirituality are overflowing today with thousands of titles. Where can we begin? Some rather stringent criteria created this list of books.

First of all, I purposely restricted myself to fewer than twenty-five books just so that the list wouldn't be overpowering and an embarrassment of riches.

Second, I have included only books that I have read myself or whose authors I know.

Third, only books available in paperback have been listed.

Finally, I have included only books that I believe will be helpful and important to a person who has worked through the present book; thus many great spiritual classics have been passed over because they don't speak easily to beginners.

General

Popenoe, Chris. *Books for Inner Development: The Yes Guide.* Random House, 1976. This is *the* bibliography in this field. A wonderful treasure trove of the available material, arranged in over seventy topics from alchemy to yoga.

Progoff, Ira. *At a Journal Workshop.* Dialogue House, 1975. *The* book on journal keeping as a growth process. Especially helpful for supplementing and deepening the journal work begun in the present book. Also very helpful for such topics as writing and creating autobiographies, dream work, dialogue with persons.

Meditation

Fox, Matthew. *On Becoming a Musical, Mystical Bear: Spirituality American Style.* Paulist, 1976. A refreshing and very nontraditional look at Western spirituality. Fox focuses upon two movements of the spiritual life—the movement toward mysticism, and the movement toward prophecy (or radical social change).

Johnston, William. *Silent Music: The Science of Meditation.* Harper & Row, 1974. A survey of the kinds of meditation as well as the scientific studies of meditation going on today, by a Jesuit priest who has spent most of his ministry in Japan and has an intimate familiarity with the Zen traditions. The chapters on friendship, intimacy, and healing are the best to be found anywhere.

LeShan, Lawrence. *How to Meditate.* Bantam, 1974. A little handbook that with great simplicity teaches how to meditate, gives a survey of all the different meditation practices, and has a chapter on the obstacles to meditation.

Kelsey, Morton. *The Other Side of Silence.* Paulist, 1976. This book focuses upon image meditation. Kelsey claims with good reason that this is the traditional Christian discipline of meditation, and his book succeeds in dusting off the cobwebs and misunderstandings from meditation upon images and stories. Especially useful as a supplement to our material on prayer as story.

Tulku, Tarthang. *Gesture of Balance.* Dharma, 1976. A sometimes difficult but always rewarding book that talks about meditation and especially about the place of meditation in life and meditation as life. Written by a Tibetan Buddhist lama who lives in Berkeley and is transmitting his great spiritual heritage to Westerners in terms we can appreciate and understand.

Body Work

Arica Institute. *Psychocalisthenics.* Simon & Schuster, 1976. This combination of exercises, including Yoga work, breathing, western calisthenics, brings the human body, spirit, and mind together into a harmonious foundation for spiritual work.

Déchanet, J. M. *Christian Yoga.* Harper & Row, 1960. One of the most helpful books on Yoga for Westerners because Déchanet is more concerned with the spiritual aspects of Yoga discipline than just with the stretching and exercise side of the practice.

Huang, Al. *Embrace the Tiger, Return to Mountain.* Real People Press, 1973. A book on Tai Chi that, like the Yoga book, is more concerned with the inner experience of Tai Chi than with teaching the bare routines.

Lowen, Alexander. *Bioenergetics.* Penguin Books, 1975. The founder of Bioenergetics, a Reichian body therapy, here explains how the body is intimately related to the spirit, and along the way gives different exercises that enable us to experience the truth of what he says.

Tulku, Tarthang. *Kum Nye.* Dharma, 1978. The Tibetan lama explains and illustrates the system of Tibetan Yoga that is used to relax the person for meditation.

Spiritual Tools

Johnston, William, translator. *The Cloud of Unknowing.* Doubleday, 1973. A great Western spiritual classic and guide for the beginner in meditation and spirituality. This author provides the student with a Western mantra meditation and describes the ups and downs of the spiritual path.

Metzner, Ralph. *Maps of Consciousness.* Macmillan, 1971. The author shows how various esoteric traditions (including astronomy, Tarot, and I Ching) provide maps and guidance for the spiritual work.

Art and Music

Bonny, Helen, and Louis Savary. *Music and Your Mind.* Harper & Row, 1973. This is the one exception to my paperback-only rule because it is the only book I know that deals with music as prayer, and it is well worth its price (not really expensive). Includes many practical suggestions on ways to pray and expand consciousness through music.

Richards, M. C. *Centering in Pottery, Poetry and the Person.* Wesleyan University Press, 1962. Simply a beautiful book to enjoy and be inspired by.

Sports and Dance

deSola, Carla. *Learning through Dance.* Paulist, 1974. Develops the spiritual dimensions that dance can release in us and offers a number of step-by-step dances.

Leonard, George. *The Ultimate Athlete.* Avon, 1977. Talks about the spiritual dimensions of sport. Also includes directions for non-competitive sports and games.

Story and Dreams

Dunne, John. *A Search for God in Time and Memory.* Notre Dame, 1977. One of the most original contemporary theologians looks at the life story in terms of what it reveals about God. Difficult but very rewarding.

Garfield, Patricia. *Creative Dreaming.* Random House, 1974. Covers all aspects of dreams: learning to remember them, how to record them, how to be aware when you are dreaming, and finally how to program your dreams and dream what you want.

Shah, Idries. *Nasrudin.* Dutton, 1971. A collection of Sufi teaching stories centering on the figure of Nasrudin, the holy fool. They are both delightfully funny and mind expanding.

Persons

Downing, George. *The Massage Book*. Random House, 1972. The complete how-to-do-it-in-all-its-varieties book.

Schutz, William. *Joy*. Grove Press, 1967. The original encounter book, filled with different games and exercises in interpersonal communication.

Index

Adam and Eve, 129
Aikido, 67, 99
Almsgiving, *see* Fasting and almsgiving
Angels, idea of, 65, 80, 91
Anger during meditation, 50
Aristotle, 113
Art and music, experiences of, 87–94
  meditation to, 47
  powers of imagination, 90–92
  praying, 92–94
  visual arts, 89–90
Astrology, 83, 84–85
Attention, the, meditation on, 30–31
Augustine, 124
Autobiographical turning points, story
  prayer and, 125–126
Awareness, walking with, 98

Bach, Johann Sebastian, 41
Beethoven, Ludwig van, 33
Blake, William, 91
Body awareness, developing, 70–71
Body and sexuality, 132–133
Breath, the, meditation on, 28
  posture and, 28–30
Buddha, 3
Buddhism, 20, 140

Calisthenics, 67
Camera, nature walk and, 109–110
Candle, meditation with, 55
Castenada, Carlos, 64
Centeredness, body work, 61–64
  below the navel, 62

exercise, 63–64
finding, 62
head and brain, 61
heart, 61–62
spiritual journey and, 62–63
Chopin, Frédéric, 41
Christianity, 32, 65, 69, 78, 82, 119,
  140
Collage, dream, 123
Communication, 88
Concentration, cultivating, 49–55
  avoiding judgments and criticisms,
    51–52
  being gentle but firm, 49–50
  defined, 53–54
  expanding versus narrowing, 54–55
  giving up expectations, 52–53
  meditation with a candle, 55
  temptations to give up, 50–51
Confessions (Augustine), 124
Consciousness, 31, 52, 53, 55, 65, 107
  God-, 79
  working on, 76–78
Conversation and listening, 134–136
Conversion, experience of, 9–10
Creating stories, 126–127
Czerny, Karl, 41

Dance, 99, 100–102
Dante, 124
David, King, 100
Decision, time for, 27–28
Depression, 11
Devils, The (motion picture), 132

Dialogue, 136–137
Discerning the spirit, notion of, 80–85
Discipline, 51, 67, 71, 78
Distractions, 18–19, 68–69
Divine Comedy (Dante), 124
Dream diary, 38
Dreams, 38, 39
    collage, 123
    expanding, 122–123
    interviews, 121
    remembering, 120–121
    role playing with, 121–122
Drug culture, 66

Ego training, 78–79
Elijah the prophet, 67
Energy body, 64–66
    teaching of Don Juan, 64–65
Energy fields, prayer of nature and,
    108–109
Enjoying prayer, 14–19
Erhard, Werner, 2
EST, 2
Exercises, cultivating, 41–85
    concentration, 49–55
    idea of centeredness, 63–64
    physical peace, 56–71
    silence, 41–48
    spiritual peace, 72–85
Expanding dreams, 122–123
Expanding versus narrowing concentra-
    tion, 54–55
Expectations, giving up, 52–53
Experiences, prayer, 39
Experimental principle, 26–31
    meditation on the attention, 30–31
    meditation on the breath, 28–30
    time to decide, 27–28

Fall, the, Christian myth of, 21
Fasting and almsgiving, 69–70
Fifth Symphony (Beethoven), 33
Flexibility, 27
Freud, Sigmund, 16, 121

Gentle, but firm, 49–50
Gifts, prayer, 39–40
Golf, 69, 98

Haiku, 111
Hanon, 41

Hare Krishna, 1–2, 138
Harris, Frank, 124
Hatha Yoga, 100, 133
Healing, experiences of, 10
Health, 10–11
Heartbeat, 46
Holy Spirit, 137

I Ching, 83–84
Ignatius of Loyola, 76, 80
Illness and healing, 10–11
Imagination, powers of, 90–92
Imaginative principle, 32–35
    meditation of thousand-petaled lotus,
        34–35
    poverty of pornography, 33–34
Imitation of Christ, The, 32
Inertia, 16–17
Initiation stories, 114–116

Jesus, 3, 53, 77, 99, 100, 113, 116, 118,
    119, 139, 141, 142–143
Jogging, 69, 103
John the Baptist, 100
John of the Cross, 15
Journal principle, 36–40
    dream diary, 38
    keeping a record, 36–37
    life diary, 37–38
    prayer diary, 38–39
    prayer experiences, 39
    prayer gifts, 39–40
    using the journal, 37
Judaism, 113
Jung, Carl G., 121

Kant, Immanuel, 52
Kum Nye (or Tibetan) relaxation Yoga,
    60, 67–68, 69
    essence of, 68

Lent, 70
Lewis, C. S., 134
Life diary, 37–38
Life stories, 123–125
Living in the present, 5
Lotus flower, meditation and, 34–35

Mantra meditation, 47–48, 53
Marriage, sacrament of, 129

Masochism, 78
Massage, 65, 133–134
Meditation, 2, 39, 57, 69
    anger and, 50
    on the attention, 30–31
    on the breath, 28
    expectations, 52–53
    learning to meditate, 51–52
    mirror, 129–132
    to music, 47
    on noise, 46
    posture, 28–30
    story prayer, 116
    temptations to give up, 50–51
    of the thousand-petaled lotus, 34–35
    walking as, 104–108
Mirror meditation, 129–132
Moon, Reverend, 1
Moses, 113
Motives, examination of, 4–5
Mount Rainier, 110
Mount Sinai, 99, 113
Mountain climbing, 98–100
Music, see Art and music
My Life and Loves (Harris), 124

Nature, prayer with, 104–111
    camera and, 109–110
    energy fields, 108–109
    haiku, 111
    review of experience, 110–114
    walking, 104–108
        attentiveness, 106–107
        opening the senses, 107–108
Newman, Cardinal John Henry, 135
Noise, cultivating silence and, 41–48
    external noise (coming to terms with),
        44–45
    Mantra meditation, 47–48
    meditation to music, 47
    meditation on noise, 46
    porous body, 46–47
    silencing the noise, 45–46
    too much noise, 42–44

Olympic Games, 56, 95–96
Om, 47
Opening the senses (walking medita-
    tion), 107–108
Openness, 26–31

Opera, 89
Originality, 32–35

Paul (apostle), 82–83
Personal parables, 119
Persons, praying of, 129–137
    body and sexuality, 132–133
    conversation and listening, 134–136
    dialogue, 136–137
    massage, 133–134
    mirror meditation, 129–132
Physical peace, cultivating, 56–71
    body prayer, 58–59
    centeredness, 61–64
    developing body awareness, 70–71
    energy body, 64–66
    exotic experiences and, 66–69
    fasting and almsgiving, 69–70
    reasons for, 56–58
    by reclaiming the body, 58
    spiritual journey as guide, 58–61
    Yoga, 57–58, 59, 60, 67, 69
Plato, 65
Pleasure principle, 14–19
    distractions, 18–19
    experience of saints, 15–16
    inertia, 16–17
    scheduling time to pray, 19
    self-motivation, 18
Poetry, 127–128
Pornography, poverty of, 33–34
Porous body, cultivating silence and,
    46–47
Posture, meditation, 28–30
Prayer:
    exercises, 41–85
        concentration, 49–55
        physical peace, 56–71
        silence, 41–48
        spiritual peace, 72–85
    experience of, 87–137
        art and music, 87–94
        nature, 104–111
        people, 129–137
        sports, 95–103
        story worlds, 112–128
    habits, 14–40
        being original, 32–35
        enjoying prayer, 14–19
        keeping a record, 36–40

openness, 26–31
seriousness, 20–25
principles of, 1–13
  examining motives, 4–5
  present moment for prayer, 6–8
  right time to begin, 5–6
  spirituality, 1–4
  taking stock, 8–12
  using the book as a personal guide,
    12–13
Prayer contract, 25
Prayer diary, 38–39, 71
Prayer experiences, 39
Prayer experiment, time consideration
  for, 5–6
Prayer gifts, 39–40, 111
Present moment for prayer, suitability
  of, 6–8
Psychocalisthenics, 67

Recordkeeping, 36–40
Relaxation, 54–55, 73–76
  techniques for, 75–76
Religious traditions, story and, 113
Requiem (Verdi), 88
Rimpoche, Tarthang Tulku, 140–142
Role playing with dreams, 121–122
Roth, Philip, 33
Routine, 5
Russell, Ken, 132

Saints, experience of, 15–16
Samsara, experience of, 20
Scheduling time to pray, 19
  creating, 22–25
Seashore, sound of, 46
Second Vatican Council, 133
Self-hypnosis, 75
Self-motivation, 18
Self-pity, 11, 17
Serious, being, 20–25
Sexuality, 132–133
Shakespeare, William, 117
Silence, cultivating, 41–48
Soko Gokai sect, 2
Soul, 65
Spiritual journey, how to use the book,
  12–13
Spiritual peace, cultivating, 72–85
  consciousness, 76–78

by discerning the spirit, 80–85
ego training, 78–79
relaxation, 73–76
Spiritual work, 2
Spirituality, 1–4
Sports, 56, 69
  prayer of, 95–103
    dance, 100–102
    guidelines for praying, 102–103
    obstacles to, 95–97
    as spiritual discipline, 97–98
    Tai Chi and mountain climbing,
      98–100
    tennis and gold, 98
    walking with awareness, 98
Star Wars (motion picture), 65–66, 98,
  131
Story prayer, 112–128
  autobiographical turning points,
    125–126
  creating from imagination, 126–127
  dreams, 120–123
    collage, 123
    expanding, 122–123
    interviews, 121
    remembering, 120–121
    role playing with, 121–122
  of initiation, 114–116
  life stories, 123–125
  meditation, 116
  personal parables, 119–120
  poetry, 127–128
  and religion, 113
  storytelling, 117–118
  that teach, 113–114
Sufi tradition, 115
Swimming, 69

Tai Chi discipline, 67, 69, 98–100, 103
Taking stock, 8–12
Tarot cards, 83–84
Teaching stories, 113–114
Teachings of Don Juan, The (Castenada),
  64
Ten Commandments, 99
Tennis, 69, 98
Tension, as an obstacle, 54, 73, 74
Thousand-petaled lotus, meditation of,
  34–35
Tibetan Buddhism, 3

Transcendental meditation, 2
Trinity, 137

University of California at Los Angeles
  (UCLA), 64

Verdi, Giuseppe, 88
Visual arts, experience of, 89–90
Vocational decisions, 9

Walking, 69
Walking meditation, 104–108
  attentiveness, 106–107
  opening the senses, 107–108

Work Principle, 20–25
  creating a schedule, 22–25
  fallen life, 20–21
  and pleasure, 21–22
  prayer contract, 25

Yin and *yang*, concept of, 98–99
Yoga, 3, 17, 57–58, 59, 60, 67, 69, 100
Young Men's Christian Association
  (YMCA), 67

Zen in the Art of Archery, 98
Zen and the Art of Motorcycle Maintenance,
  98
Zen Buddhism, 3, 17, 28